When Sean Became James

Martin McNamara

SunRise

SunRise

First published in Great Britain in 2022 by SunRise

SunRise Publishing Ltd
124 City Road
London EC1V 2NX

ISBN 978-1-9144892-7-3

A CIP catalogue record for this book is available from the British
Library.

Typeset in Minion Pro and Impact.

Contents

Success is the ability to go from one failure to another with no loss of enthusiasm.

Winston Churchill

1 What's in a name?

The lead actor sits at a kidney-shaped gaming table, his back to the camera. The crisp white cuffs and collar of his shirt peak out from the impeccably tailored jacket. The film set has been made to look like a high-end casino. Coiffured ladies in gowns and pearls and their tuxedoed male companions gather around the table, watching as our hero plays a tense, high-stakes game of *Chemin de fer*, a version of baccarat. His opponent, seated directly opposite him, is beautiful, brunette and aloof; dressed in a daring, off one shoulder scarlet gown. The croupier switches effortlessly between French and English as he oversees the match. The casino, Le Cercle, built from scratch at Pinewood Studios, is based it on Les Ambassadeurs Club. The real casino, some miles away in the heart of Mayfair, London, had a supporting role in the origin story of the film, but more of that later.

The set designer had been allocated a very modest budget to create and build the interior sets needed for the film. He'd spent most of the money on an impressive, and realistic looking nuclear facility and the stylish lair of the film's central villain. Despite the lack of funds, he's managed to do a pretty good job re-creating the kind of elite club the lead character would enjoy. Today's shoot is particularly important. This will be the public's first introduction to a new film hero. Many cinemagoers will already know the character from a stream of best-selling novels but how will they react to the screen version?

The film's production team has only recently returned from Jamaica, having completed six weeks of location shooting. There had been problems. Bad weather had messed with what was already a tight schedule. There were frustrating delays in filming caused by the late arrival of key pieces of equipment, props and some of the crew. The island had never been used as a location for a major film before. The locals they hired were unused to either the demands of location filming, or the long, working days and nights. A few of the scenes in the script had to be scrapped due to lack of time or budget. The production team knew they would have to find ways to pick up the shots at Pinewood, or else cover for the missing scenes in the edit suite.

Nevertheless, their leading man had acquitted himself well in Jamaica. Many of the key, dramatic elements of their story had already been filmed, and they looked good in the rushes. The hero had been set upon by multiple villains. He'd narrowly escaped death, several times. He had seduced beautiful women, usually only shortly after meeting them. The location crew had captured exterior shots that would be part of the big, climatic destruction of the antagonist's secret base — pleasingly chaotic scenes filled with billowing black smoke and lots of extras diving into the water to save themselves. They had filmed the closing shot of the movie where — against all odds — the hero and his beautiful new girlfriend escape to sea in a small dinghy.

In the pre-production planning for the film, there had been misgivings about the casting of the lead. These came from the studio heads and financiers, as well as the author of the original novels and from the film's director. Even now, on location, the film's pair of producers were hearing worrying rumours that executives at the studio financing the production were already dismissing their film as that 'Limey spy movie'. But they were betting that when the execs saw the footage of their actor on Caribbean beaches, dispatching enemies and bedding lovers with equal elan, those doubts would be allayed. Their carefully chosen lead had slipped into his role with supreme confidence.

To save money, the director had filled out some of the minor, supporting roles with local non-actors, hired in Jamaica. As the leading man advised one of his new, and very nervous, co-stars who was making her acting debut, 'If you look the part, self-confidence will arrive.' He was certainly looking the part. But right now, seated in the Pinewood set built to look like a casino and dressed immaculately: suit from Saville Row tailor Anthony Sinclair and shirt from Turnbull & Asser of Jermyn Street, that self-confidence seemed to have deserted him.

His director had made the creative decision to steal the screen introduction of his lead from another film. *Juarez* was an American, historical drama made just before the Second World War. The cinema audience sees the back of the head and close ups of the hands of the film's star, Paul Muni, before the camera finally reveals his face. It's a clever trick, building the audience's anticipation before revealing the key player in the story.

On the Pinewood set, this lead character is winning repeatedly against his beautiful adversary. The camera closes in on his masculine hands as he deals fresh cards, the perfectly manicured nails. The rim of his Rolex 6538, known as Big Crown in watch aficionado circles, just visible under the crisp, white shirt cuff. It's a very expensive piece of timekeeping, even by the standards of 1962, but it is the perfect watch for this debonaire hero. The production team had spent a small fortune on ensuring their lead has a beautifully tailored wardrobe, and they didn't have a big budget to start with. In the end, one of the producers takes the Big Crown off his own wrist and hands it to the lead actor to wear for the duration of the shoot.

The camera lingers on the back of the actor's head. The strong, capable neck; short, neat, thick dark hair. Then back to his hands, casually flipping over cards to win another round. Despite her mounting losses, and the obvious concerns of the observers around the table, his sexy opponent coolly meets his gaze and ups the betting. The leading man conceals any surprise at her apparent recklessness. He takes out a gun metal cigarette case. Another close-up on those masculine hands as he opens the case and removes a cigarette.

'I admire your courage, Miss...?' he says, his face still off-camera.

'Trench,' she replies, nonchalantly, 'Sylvia Trench,' before adding, 'I admire your luck, Mr...?' Finally, the camera lands on the leading actor's handsome face. The cigarette hangs from his lips, insolently. He lights it with a black, oxidised Ronson lighter.

'Bond,' a measured pause. 'Sean Bond.'

'And Cut!'

There follows another couple of takes, and each time Sean Connery manages to mangle his own name with that of his character.

'I'd known Sean for years and I'd never seen him so nervous as he was on that day,' said Eunice Gayson, the actress who plays Sylvia Trench. Their director, Terence Young, is becoming exasperated. He calls for a short break in filming. Young is sophisticated and urbane. He's public school-educated and ex-military with an impressive war record. His demeanour and background are remarkably similar to those of James Bond, the fantasy character his actor is attempting — and failing — to remember the name of.

By contrast, his leading man is a one-time milkman and former coffin polisher from the rough working-class tenements of Edinburgh. Sean Connery's career path up to this point could be classed as unique, especially in the post-war British cinema where leading men with cut glass accents and drawing room manners still dominate. Thomas Connery, as his parents named him, made his stage debut participating in bodybuilding contests. That arena was not a place where he felt comfortable, but it was an opportunity where he figured he could exploit what nature and his parents had given him. The tall stature. A strong, muscular build, and a rugged, commanding handsomeness. It offered a potential escape route from the drudgery of low paid, dead-end jobs that seemed the lot of an uneducated, young man from the slums of the Fountainbridge district of his hometown.

The world of bodybuilding, where grown men spend their days rubbing Vaseline into each other's nipples, was not a happy fit for this intelligent, no-nonsense Scot. However, while attending a contest in London, he landed another gig that required tall, good-looking men. A place in the chorus line of a touring production of the musical *South Pacific*. The part didn't stretch his abilities. 'Although I didn't have a voice, couldn't dance,' remembered Connery, 'I could look good standing there.'

However, the job was enough to give him a taste for the stage, and the acting bug. More theatre work followed: larger parts and a few speaking roles. Then small appearances in television dramas and low-budget British films. Usually, he was cast as some kind of thug, or a bouncer, which just happened to have been one of his many dead-end jobs back in Edinburgh. What should have been his big screen break-through came several years before Bond. Connery was put under contract by the major American studio, 20th Century Fox. To kick off the relationship with his new bosses, he was cast in a 1958 wartime drama, *Another Time, Another Place*. Sean took the role of a married BBC reporter who has an affair with an older American correspondent, played by a genuine screen goddess, Lana Turner. His character dies early in the story, but it is still the leading male role.

Unfortunately, the film was not the hit everyone hoped for. It is better remembered now because Turner's violent, Mafia-connected boyfriend became convinced Connery was having an affair with his girl. He flew to London, arrived on the set drunk, armed with a revolver, and ready to teach this young actor what was what. When the mobster came at him, Connery took away his gun with ease and laid him out with a single punch. Bond couldn't have handled it better.

Sean's most successful film, pre-Bond, saw him play a supporting role to a leprechaun. *Darby O'Gill and the Little People* was a whimsical Disney production about a wily old Irishman who tries to outwit the King of the Leprechauns. Connery played the handsome young lad courting the old man's daughter. It was a wholesome movie firmly aimed at the family market. The film caught the eye of Cubby Broccoli, an Italian-American film producer based in London. He was especially interested in the performance of the handsome, young supporting player with the dodgy Irish accent.

Broccoli and his new partner, Harry Saltzman, a Canadian film producer who had also landed up in post-war England, had acquired the rights to most of the James

Bond novels. Writer Ian Fleming had been churning out the spy's fictional adventures, one book a year, since the early 1950s. The producing pair made an unlikely couple. Saltzman, a no-nonsense Canadian could be demanding, scary and often just downright rude. Broccoli, by contrast, was kind and friendly to everyone. With his round frame, big open smile, and carefully cultivated gentle demeanour, more than one person referred to him as a 'teddy bear'.

Michael Caine, who in a few years would play a very different British secret agent, Harry Palmer, in a series of movies produced by Saltzman, described their competing personalities succinctly. 'They were like policemen. Cubby would light you a cigarette and Harry would smack it out of your mouth.'

They were, however, in agreement on one thing. That, with the right handling, they could take Fleming's violent, womanising, cruel and sadistic secret agent from the pages of his novels and turn him into a compelling big screen hero. The pair had a wildly, ambitious notion. If this first film was a success, they could produce a whole series of Bond movies, maybe as many as six or seven. But, back in 1961, they had been struggling to get a single film made, and time was running out on their option on the Bond stories.

The first major hurdle was finance. They both had good working relationships with some of the major Hollywood studios but for this project they found little enthusiasm. They were told the Bond novels were too violent, too sexual and — the biggest sin of all — too damned English. Eventually, United Artists agreed to back the production, but only with a budget of one million dollars. This was not a great deal of money for a thriller with glamourous foreign locations, expensive sets and big scale action sequences requiring armies of extras and special effects.

They had planned to start with an adaptation of Fleming's most recently published novel. That was before they discovered the author had created the book out of a screenplay he produced in collaboration with a couple of filmmakers. He didn't bother to inform the pair of this fact and now they were in bitter litigation with the author over the rights to the story. The producers turned instead to Fleming's sixth Bond novel, *Dr No*. This book had only one exotic location, Jamaica, and one big set piece, so would hopefully be more doable on their modest budget.

Dr No had also started life as a screenplay. This time for a proposed television show entitled *Commander Jamaica*. It never got made and Fleming, who didn't like to waste any material, adapted the story into the book. The producers knew if their first Bond flick misfired it would not only be the beginning of their franchise, but its end. They also knew the key to success was finding the exact right actor to play the agent with a licence to kill.

The list of leading men considered for the role is extensive. In the novels, Fleming describes Bond as resembling Hoagy Carmichael, a tall, languid American actor and musician who starred in a series of films in the 1940s, usually playing a pianist with a cigarette hanging from his lips.

The producers' financial backers were pushing for a big name to play Bond but Fleming's suggestion for the role, David Niven, was quickly passed on. The producers briefly considered Cary Grant, a friend of Broccoli's and best man at his wedding, but Cubby knew that Grant wouldn't be interested in doing more than one film. And anyway, his fee for his recent hit, *North By Northwest*, was equal to about half their entire budget. James Mason was interested but worried about being typecast and would only sign on for two films. The Irish American actor Patrick McGoohan, a devout Catholic, discussed the role with the pair but eventually turned them down because of the 'immoral' nature of the Fleming stories, and the lead character. 'I thought there was too much emphasis on sex and violence,' McGoohan explained later. 'Would you like your son to grow up like James Bond?'

Other names: Rex Harrison, Michael Redgrave, Richard Todd, Rod Taylor and Trevor Howard, were apparently considered and had either passed on the project or were passed over. Another potential Bond who was not available was a young television actor called Roger Moore, but Broccoli thought he was a 'shade too pretty' anyway. To build a sense of anticipation around their upcoming film, the producers conspired with the *Daily Express* to run a competition to find the man to play Bond. There were a thousand entries and a male model, Peter Anthony, won. Despite being given a screen test, this non-actor was never going to get the gig. What the producers really wanted was an actor who was experienced but not an established star; one they could craft into the role, who would be happy to sign up for a possible series of films and would not be too expensive. When *Dr No*, finally became a success and made Connery a bona fide star, Sean would caustically remark that Saltzman and Broccoli (with whom he had many run-ins) would have happily played the role themselves if they could have, just to save the expense of paying him.

There was another, key reason why they felt they needed a new face. Fleming had created a distinctly English agent, a product of a public school education and privileged background, much like his own. However, with his novels, the author had wanted to rebel against the traditional, class-bound British heroes. James Bond was not your typical adventurer, there was none of the fair play and gentlemanly behaviour of a Bulldog Drummond or a

Biggles. This was an agent for a post-world-war, post-Empire Britain, a nation still trying to find its position in an uncomfortably changing world. A world which was getting more uncertain, darker and threatening. In planning his books, Fleming took inspiration from a slew of bleak, cynical, American pulp fiction novels including the film noir stories of Dashiell Hammett and Raymond Chandler. He was a particular fan of Mickey Spillane's hardboiled, misanthropic, and frankly psychotic detective, Mike Hammer.

The film's two producers, both migrants to England, who stood at arms' length from the country's stultifying class system, recognised that Fleming was creating a new kind of British hero. Yes, Bond was devoted to Queen and Country, but he was also unchivalrous, arrogant and, when it was needed, violent and cold blooded. He came with this special status, a 'licence of kill'.

The nature of Bond's character had already earned Ian Fleming a great deal of criticism from people who disapproved of his apparent lack of morality. But Cubby Broccoli recognised what the author was trying to achieve with Bond: 'This is the Fleming formula. You don't see Bond kill for the sake of killing, he always kills in self-defence (but) it's very un-British and, also, pretty un-American. It's not like in a Western, where the hero waits for the other man to draw. Bond isn't equipped that way. He's not taking any chances.'

Bringing that violence to the big screen would earn the producers their own share of condemnation. They were ready for their critics. 'We live in an age of violence,' said Harry Saltzman. 'James Bond epitomises the age of violence. He is today's Tarzan, today's Superman. We live in a very amoral age and Bond is a product of that age.'

But, back in 1961. the producers were not tangling with

those gritty moral issues. What they needed right now was an actor who was masculine enough to realistically enact the violence of Bond. They needed someone with the sexual magnetism to be a believable ladies' man. And they needed someone who could bring to the screen those dangerous aspects of Bond: his ruthlessness, his coldness, his sadism, and still, at the same time, make the audience root for him.

Trevor Howard, best remembered as the thoroughly decent doctor struggling to do the right thing in *Brief Encounter*, was not quite the right fit. What they were really looking for was a new type of British leading man. Saltzman had made his name in the late 1950s producing gritty, British kitchen sink dramas, notably *Saturday Night and Sunday Morning* and *Look Back in Anger*. In doing so, he helped the careers of a new breed of powerful, working-class actors including the films' leads, Albert Finney and Richard Burton.

Broccoli and Saltzman started to sift through the ranks of this new, exciting generation of actors and, in going for a lesser-known performer, they were in accord with Ian Fleming. What the author really wanted was for his hero James Bond to be the star name in the movie, and not the actor who played him. Broccoli was impressed by Connery's performance in *Darby O'Gill*, at least, impressed enough to run the film past his wife, who was even more enthusiastic. Connery had a certain something, said Dana Broccoli, and she became his earliest, and most enthusiastic, advocate for the Bond role.

Cubby was still undecided, although he felt Connery acquitted himself well in the film's big third act fight scene. He had a tough job convincing his fellow producer to consider Sean for the role, but Saltzman eventually agreed to bring Connery in for a meeting at their London office.

WHEN SEAN BECAME JAMES

By this time, the Scottish actor had grown disillusioned with the type of film roles he was being offered: too many two-dimensional parts as a heavy. After his brief, and less than happy interlude with Hollywood, he had turned back to British theatre and television, working his way through major roles from Chekhov to Shakespeare and Ibsen. His performances were picking up good reviews. People were starting to take note of Sean Connery for his acting skills rather than his looks. Having fallen, pretty much by accident, into this acting lark, Connery was determined to learn his craft. He'd left school at 14 and was now making up for his lack of formal education. He was teaching himself by reading Joyce, Tolstoy, Proust, Thomas Wolfe and others, hungry for knowledge and new experiences.

As well as tackling the big classical roles, he was soaking up the wisdom of his more experienced and better educated acting and writing mates. Connery read a few of the Fleming books and had his own definite ideas on how the secret agent should be played, and why he would be the best man to take on the job. He made a bold choice in his approach to his meeting with the two producers. Another actor might have dressed in a tuxedo to show how he could pull off the classic Bond look. Connery turned up in his usual 'actor not presently working' attire, which was dirt cheap army surplus gear. He took control of the meeting immediately, telling the producers how they should be thinking about screen Bond and what they needed to do to make the film a success. For emphasis he banged his fist on the table.

When Cubby mentioned setting up a screen test, Sean told him, as far as he was concerned, he would not be willing to do a test for the role. 'I'm past that,' he said, with finality. They could take him or leave him. When he left the meeting, the astonished producers weren't quite sure what had happened.

Dana called her husband and Saltzman to the window so they could watch Connery walk away, across South Audley Street, to his girlfriend's parked car. She recognised what millions of women would soon see in darkened cinemas around the world. The sensual, graceful way the actor carried himself. 'He moves like a panther,' she said.

Connery's display of arrogance and virility paid off. Both producers were now convinced he had the qualities to be their Bond. Over the decade since publication of Fleming's first book, *Casino Royale*, multiple attempts had been made to bring Bond to the screen. All had floundered, much to Fleming's frustration. A one-hour movie had been produced of that first novel for CBS in the States, but this American reimagining of 'Jimmie Bond' impressed nobody, least of all Fleming. Other attempts by the author to work with writers, directors and producers over the past decade had ended in failure.

Saltzman had paid him a much welcome $50,000 for six months' rights to virtually all of the Bond canon. Fleming was happy to take the money but had good reason to suspect this was all going to be another disappointment. His worst suspicions seemed confirmed when he was introduced to the actor the producers had in mind to play Bond. 'He's nothing but an overgrown stuntman,' he moaned. Connery was working class, uneducated, Scottish and, what was worse for a snob like Fleming, 'unrefined'. He was, in short, everything that Bond was not.

Broccoli and Saltzman were not going to be put off by Fleming's disapproval. Their bigger problem was the executives at United Artists. The names of a lot of reliable British stars had been thrown around by the producers for this role and the execs were not going to be happy if their million-dollar investment was going to rely on this little-known actor. Connery's film career had been patchy.

His Scottish accent had been tempered since leaving Edinburgh, but still didn't suggest a suave, privately educated English special agent. And if that weren't enough, he was going bald. Despite Connery's insistence that he would not do a screen test, Broccoli and Saltzman tricked him into taking part in one, saying they needed to test him against actresses being considered for roles in the film. When the screen test was sent to United Artists, the response was short and blunt: keep searching.

But the stubborn New Yorker and fearsome Canadian were not going to be swayed: they held firm, Connery was their man. Yes, he was a rough diamond but one that they were confident they could polish up. When Connery met Fleming, he listened patiently as the author gave him his advice on how to play Bond. 'What was it he called me, or told somebody? That I was an "over-developed stunt man"', remembered Connery 'He never said it to me. When I did eventually meet him, he was very interesting, erudite and a snob, a real snob.'

Connery had every reason to be particularly sensitive of any kind of condescension. This was a man who was acutely aware of his lack of education, especially now, when he was mixing with a sophisticated and erudite set in the creative hub of London. To compensate, he became a sponge, soaking up the books, theatre and ideas he never been exposed to growing up in Edinburgh. He investigated the different acting techniques, including the Method. He had signed up as a student of Yat Malmgren, a Swedish dance teacher who was popular with this new generation of actors in London. Yat taught him how to move, how to position his body in space in such a way as to make for maximum dramatic impact in any given scene.

Sean was a willing student who wanted to learn from anyone who could teach him something useful. And, when he was eventually signed up for the Bond role, he found the perfect teacher to educate him in the ways of a sophisticated secret agent. The two north American producers were agreed the project needed a British director to keep the Bond story close to its roots. Terence Young was at least the fifth director they approached, and the only one to say yes. At first, Young was another figure who felt Connery was completely wrong for the role. He had worked with him a few years earlier on a film. Connery only had a small role, and the director had liked him well enough. However, when he was informed of the producers' decision to cast Connery as Bond, he buried his head in his head and moaned: 'Disaster! Disaster! Disaster!'

Young had been pushing for the Shakespearean actor, Richard Johnson, and although he considered Connery to be a good actor, he thought he lacked the sophistication for the part of Bond. But, ever the team player, the director threw himself into the job of assisting Sean into his new persona. As well as the public school and military background, Young shared other characteristics with the fictional Bond. He was tall, elegant, attractive, erudite and irresistible to women. He enjoyed the finer things in life and was utterly at ease in high society, or anywhere else.

Young had a devil may care attitude to life. Cast and crew on his location shoots grew used to being invited to champagne and caviar parties thrown by the director, at his own expense. 'Terence should have played Bond,' said Connery, acknowledging how much he owed him in finding his way into the role.

Young took Sean to his personal tailor, Anthony Sinclair, and got him suited. The master tailor cut the cloth of Bond's suit so that the holstered weapon under his left arm would not affect the all-important line of the jacket. Then Young told the perplexed Scot to sleep in his expensive new attire; this was how the upper classes made sure their clothes fitted. The actor was astonished to wake up in the morning and find that the suit he had slept in had kept its shape perfectly.

Then, with Sean all dressed up, Terence escorted him to the classiest restaurants in London. He taught him how to order food, and how to eat the exotic dishes, and which cutlery to use with which course. He tutored him on how to order wine, and when to send it back. He taught him how to light his cigarette, how to light a woman's cigarette, and how to walk across a room. He explained the rules of play at the casino tables, and the equally important etiquette of this select, high stakes gambling world.

Lois Maxwell, who would play Miss Moneypenny in *Dr No*, and a further 13 Bond films, said: 'Terence took Sean under his wing. He took him to dinner, showed him how to walk, how to talk, even how to eat.' Young tutored his pupil away from the decidedly working-class habit of moving his hands around when he talked. The lessons worked. Connery could now walk across a crowded casino wearing a tuxedo as if he had been born into this world. The only criticism pedantic class experts could find was the, apparently, non-upper crust way Connery buttoned his jacket in the film. Many of the cast, when they saw the completed film in the cinema, concluded that Sean Connery was doing a very good Terence Young impersonation.

Other preparations were made in London before they could head off to shoot in Jamaica. Sean was fitted with two wigs to cover his receding hairline. One to use when he was dry and on land and the other for when he was in, or coming out of, the water. He was also persuaded by Terence to have his heavy eyebrows trimmed slightly. The pair's close partnership would have a measurable impact on the style of *Dr No*, and on all subsequent Bond films, if not the entire genre of action thrillers to follow.

Both Connery and Young felt Fleming's Bond was severely lacking in one key area: a sense of humour. The hero of the novels had a life filled with violence, sex, fine food, exotic wines, glamorous locations, beautiful women, demonic villains and fast cars. However, laughs were not much on display in Bond's existence. The final *Dr No* script which made its way to the location shooting had kept faithful to much of the novel's plot, but the screenwriters had injected some of that much needed humour. On the set, both the director and his actor started to look at ways to slip some more fun into Bond.

Terence encouraged Sean to ad lib and introduce comic asides to provide light relief, especially after scenes of violence, tension and sex. Bond is met at the airport in Jamaica by an assassin, Mr Jones, pretending to be his chauffeur. Bond figures out the deception and, on a dusty side road, he battles the assassin. When Mr Jones kills himself with a poisoned cigarette, Bond dumps his body in the back of the convertible and drives on to the Governor's mansion. He pulls up outside the building with a dead man propped up in the backseat. As he hops out of the vehicle Connery ad-libbed to the waiting police officer: 'Sergeant, make sure he doesn't get away.'

Young loved the line and so it stayed in the film. He worked with, and encouraged, his actor to bring more of that humour into the role. The director wasn't just trying to have fun. He knew the violence and sexual content of the film would likely bring them into conflict with the censors. He had learned that tempering fight scenes, brutal murders, and sexual content with a dose of humour and witty one-liners would help the film avoid an 'R' rating. Falling foul of the censors would greatly restrict potential audiences and the filmmakers' ability to make back their money.

Young's coaching worked, with Sean effortlessly bringing Bond to life on the screen. However, this success was not an actor and his director working in isolation. The creation of the enduring screen Bond which would set the template for all the films across the sixty-year (and counting) franchise, could only have happened because this unique group of men, from wildly different backgrounds, came together at this particular moment in time, and created a unique movie. It was something Barbara Broccoli, Cubby's daughter and a current producer of the Bond films, would recognise years later: 'The original filmmakers were Cubby and Harry, Ian Fleming, Terence Young and Sean Connery. They all created something extraordinary. They changed cinema history. They pushed the envelope.'

Such notions were far from the reality of shooting this low-budget, small fantasy British spy flick. Even Connery wasn't expecting much to come from his starring role in *Dr No*. 'It's just another job,' he told a fellow jobbing actor at the time. 'Then I'll be waiting for the phone to ring as usual.'

Eunice Gayson, who would be the first in a very long line of Bond girls, said *Dr No* was a revolution for British actresses. 'Thank goodness for *Dr No* and the Bond movies,' said Eunice, 'because Terence Young wasn't afraid of woman. He said to me: 'I want you because you're sexy. In those days to be sexy on screen, the British screen, that was out. You didn't look sexy in a British film. It was pathetic really.'

But, right now, on the set at Pinewood, none of this is on anyone's agenda. Terence Young, his lead actor and the nervous producers have but one focus: getting this scene performed correctly and in the can. This is a crucial moment. It will be the introduction to audiences of Sean, as James. And you don't get a second chance at a first impression.

Connery is angry at himself for messing it up. Eunice remembered: 'By this time everyone was nervous, the director was nervous, the cast were nervous, and Sean above all was nervous, bless his heart. The first takes, "Bond, James Bond" didn't come that easy. I was seconded to take him into another room and have a drink or two.' The two actors sat down, shared a few glasses of whisky and talked quietly. 'As he had been on the wagon for several months for this shooting,' said Eunice. 'I was worried how it would affect him. And it did affect him, but in a nice way, because he came back full of the Bond image.'

They returned to the set where the director and crew prepared to shoot the scene again. The leading man parries with his beautiful opponent across the baccarat table. He again compliments the bravery of Sylvia Trench, played by Gayson. Sylvia compliments him back, on his luck, and asks his name. The camera watches him remove the untipped cigarette from his cigarette case, then cuts to the shot of his face where the cigarette hangs insolently from his lips before he lights it. 'Bond,' he says and, after an extended pause which speaks to the character's effortless self-assurance: 'James Bond.'

'And cut.' The scene is perfection.

'Every woman in the world wanted to meet James Bond after that,' said Eunice. 'Terence Young said to him "that is exactly how I want you to play Bond, just like that". And Sean said to me: "The trouble is, I don't remember what it I was I did."' The British film critic Peter Bradshaw would say of the scene: 'It is the most famous self-introduction from any character in movie history. Three cool monosyllables, surname first, a little curtly, as befits a former naval commander, and then, as if in afterthought, the first name, followed by the surname again. Connery carried it off with icily disdainful style, in full evening dress with a cigarette hanging from his lips. The introduction was a kind of challenge, or seduction, invariably addressed to an enemy. In the early '60s, Connery's James Bond was about as dangerous and sexy as it got on screen.'

Or, as director Terence Young put it: 'it was one hell of a good introduction.'

Sean Connery was so nervous during a crucial scene in *Dr No*, that Eunice Gayson, who played Sylvia Trench, was asked to take him off the set for a calming drink. It worked, and together they filmed the most memorable scene in any Bond movie.

2 A strongly marked streak of voyeurism & sadomasochism

Director Terence Young is frustrated with how filming is proceeding on the location shoot. There have been multiple delays and missed days caused by bad weather, which is just a fact of life if you're filming in the Caribbean. They also had to deal with the late arrival of some essential crew members and equipment, further messing with their already tight schedule. But now they have a few calm, perfect days to shoot the beach scenes where James Bond first meets Honey Rider, the beautiful, coral diver who emerges out of the clear blue sea, wearing just a bikini, and a knife.

The crew are set up on the finest beach in Jamaica, Laughing Waters, on the north coast of the island. The ex-pat who owns this stunning piece of real estate is notoriously private and difficult to deal with. Nonetheless, she gives permission to the filmmakers because she's a big fan of the Ian Fleming novels. The beach is standing in for coastline of Crab Key, the fictitious private island controlled by the shadowy Dr No.

The leading actor, Sean Connery, and the producers, Cubby Broccoli and Harry Saltzman, met the actress playing Honey for the first time in Jamaica. Originally,

27

back in London, Julie Christie had been considered for the role, but she'd been passed over, partially because the producers didn't think her breasts were large enough. They had been searching in vain for the right actress to play the naïve but independently minded Honey, until the moment Broccoli plucked a photo of a stunning young woman in a wet shirt out of scores of portraits, and decided she was the one.

The Swiss born model and actress Ursula Andress was based in Los Angeles, living with her husband, the actor, director, and photographer John Derek. Broccoli checked Andress out with a movie business associate in Hollywood who confirmed her outstanding beauty, but added, she had a 'voice like a Dutch comic'. They cast her anyway and without meeting her. They could always dub her in post. Ursula was sent a ticket to fly from LA to New York, and Terence Young flew out to meet her at the airport and escort her to Jamaica. The gamble paid off. Ursula would be perfect for the role, developing an easy rapport with Connery which translated effortlessly onto the screen.

And yes, her heavy accent would need to be dubbed for the final cut. One actress provided the voice for her dialogue, and another covered her rendition of *Under a Mango Tree*, sung as she examines the coral she's collected from the floor of the Caribbean Sea. This scene, where she first emerges from the water in bikini and sheathed knife, will become an iconic image of movie history. But right now, all Terence Young and his crew care about is getting the damned shot in the can.

The director has his people in place. He's discussed the scene with his two lead players, Ursula and Sean, and they are ready and on their spots. Just as he shouts 'action', four middle-aged, white people, seemingly oblivious to the production, amble down across the clean, white sands, threatening to enter the shot. Young, a former tank commander who saw action at Arnhem, is for most of the time the model of calmness and unflappability. His philosophy is always to make his film set as much fun as possible for everyone involved. But he does have a fierce temper on him. He shouts angrily at the quartet, and they duck out of sight in the dunes. The scene continues. Young yells 'cut' and the crew burst into spontaneous applause. They seem to recognise they have just witnessed something rather special. He checks with his cameraman and the rest of the team. They got the shot. No problems and he can relax a little, as the crew begin the necessary adjustments to capture the scene from a different angle.

Half an hour later, the director is strolling along the beach and in the dunes discovers the four intruders, still lying flat on their stomachs, unsure if they are allowed to move without interfering with filming or getting yelled at again. He immediately recognises one of the party: Ian Fleming, Bond's author, who has a house on the island and thought it might be fun to wander over to the set with his wife and a couple of friends. It's a minor incident and Fleming can afford to laugh it off. After all, it's been ten years, almost to the day, since he first sat down at his typewriter in his hideaway on the island and began work on the first James Bond novel. Now here he is, on the set of the first proper, cinematic production to be made featuring his special agent.

Ian Fleming was born into a family of privilege and money on 28 May 1908 in Mayfair, London. His grandfather, Robert Fleming, a native of Dundee, started working at the age of 13 as an office boy to a local merchant. From such modest circumstances Robert would build a fortune, investing in American railroads and founding a private merchant bank which would be run by the Fleming family. The Fleming clan motto is 'Let the Deed Show'. Ian's father, Valentine Fleming, who had been a Conservative MP, who would die in World War One at the Somme. His good friend Winston Churchill wrote his obituary in *The Times*.

Ian, who was devoted to his father, was nine at the time. His strong-willed mother Eve was left to raise their four sons by herself. Peter, the eldest, then Ian and Michael and Richard. Their father had left the family comfortably off, but this branch of the Flemings had been effectively disinherited from the banking fortune. Under the terms of the will, Eve, who had been a socialite and a beauty, would be disinherited if she remarried. She contented herself with a string of lovers, including the artist, Augustus John.

Eve was a dominating mother, vain and controlling of her sons' lives, especially Ian, who would have a difficult and often strained relationship with her and her attempts to manage and direct his life. He called her 'M' rather than mother. This might possibly have been the inspiration for the codename given to Bond's overbearing and disapproving paternal boss in the spy novels that would make Fleming's name. As might be expected of someone from his background, Ian was sent to Eton. He was an excellent athlete but a poor student, although he did display an aptitude for languages. He broke his nose in a football match which gave his handsome features an interesting, roguish aspect.

His tutors were already seeing and disapproving of the traits that would characterise his life. He could be arrogant and insolent, with a laziness toward anything that did not interest him. Like his fictional hero, Ian Fleming would leave Eton early, on the 'advice' of his house master. Eve, having decided that Ian would have a military career, got him enrolled into Sandhurst, the academy for future officers of the British army. His mother's plan went awry after Ian contracted a social disease from a lady in Soho and had to leave the college after less than a year.

Her next strategy for her wayward son was a career in the Foreign Office. He was packed off to a private school in Austria to improve on his language skills, which he did, when he was not chasing women, drinking, and partying. Among his liaisons was a Swiss woman called Monique that developed into something serious. But when he discussed marriage with his mother, Eve, told him if he wed this woman, she would cut him out of his inheritance. Ian duly split from Monique, but he never quite forgot her. When he got round to providing biographical details for James Bond in the novel, *You Only Live Twice*, it included the death of his parents in a skiing accident when James was 11. Bond's mother had been a beautiful Swiss woman called Monique.

Ian returned to England and sat for the Foreign Office entry exam but he failed to achieve enough of a mark to be accepted. This litany of mishaps and disappointments was all very different from that of his older brother. Ian would both look up to Peter and spent much of his life in his shadow. His elder brother excelled academically and on the sports field. He would also become a successful writer years before his brother.

Eve's next port of call for her wayward, dissolute second son was journalism. She used her connections to get him a job at the Reuters news agency and, with his now excellent language skills, he was sent to work in Berlin and Moscow. In 1933, six British employees of the Metropolitan-Vickers Electrical Company working in Russia were arrested in one of Stalin's great purges. Because he could speak Russian, Fleming would cover their trial for Reuters. He was just 25.

But there was an inner restlessness that sent him looking for yet another change of direction. Journalism simply didn't pay enough to support the kind of lifestyle that he felt he deserved. Basically, what Ian Fleming needed was a career that paid extremely well, did not consume too much of his time and allowed him to enjoy a rotating cast of girlfriends and parties and good times. Back in London he turned to the City, but found he wasn't much good at being a stockbroker. He was heading past the age of 30 and he still hadn't figured out what he was going to do with his life. Meanwhile his brother Peter was making a name for himself as an adventurer and travel writer, producing best-selling books about his journeys in Asia and South America. Then the war came over the horizon.

In 1939, Ian was back in Moscow. His cover was as a reporter for *The Times*, but he was now working for the Foreign Office. His remit was to look at ways Britain could support Soviet military and morale if, as was hoped, they came into the war against the Nazis. When the war came, Fleming joined the Royal Navy and was made personal assistant to the Director of Naval Intelligence. He became immersed in a shadowy world which, he discovered, he loved, and seemed to have some aptitude for. It was an exciting realm of espionage, black propaganda and *Boy's Own* adventures; full of madcap, daring plans to outwit the enemy by any means possible.

Working mostly from his desk at the Admiralty, Ian had finally found employment that engaged him as much as the women and the gambling tables. In June 1940, while the Germans were overrunning France, he went to Bordeaux to try to convince the French Naval Commander, Admiral Darlan, to evacuate his fleet to British ports. While there, he helped British people stranded in the country get back home. He burned files and papers at the makeshift British

A STRONGLY MARKED STREAK OF VOYEURISM & SADOMASOCHISM

Embassy so they wouldn't fall into enemy hands and apparently assisted King Zog of Albania and his family to escape to safety.

Friends had long recognised that there was a boyishness that had been part of Fleming's makeup and it was that aspect of him which was given full range by the war. He was coming up with, or assisting in, schemes that ran from the daring to the hair-brained and plain crazy. He visited a secret training camp in Canada and took part in exercises to plant limpet mines on the hull of a derelict tanker. Bond would undertake a similar mission in *Live and Let Die*. However, while on exercises he found that his nerves were not those of the fearless warrior class. Fleming might have felt frustrated by his desk bound job, but it seems like it was the most appropriate place for him. Back in London, he was promoted to Commander. He celebrated by having three gold bands adorn the custom-made cigarettes he purchased from Morland & Co, a small tobacco shop in Grosvenor Street. The cigarettes were identical to those smoked by the future, fictional Commander Bond.

Fleming assisted in the creation of the 30 Assault Unit, or 30AU, whose mission was to go deep behind enemy lines to collect intelligence and documents about German military's plans, including their rumoured nuclear programme. The unit operated independently from other departments as their mission was seen as a matter of utmost importance. He was full of admiration for the work of a German officer, Otto Skorzeny, who had revolutionised the use of intelligence and guerrilla tactics to outwit the enemy. Nothing was off limits for Otto, who would use blackmail, kidnapping and extortion to gather intelligence. He would later serve as inspiration for the character of Hugo Drax, the villain in the novel *Moonraker*.

Fleming may not have seen much field action, but his

wartime experience gave him a unique grounding in the inner workings of naval intelligence. He was helping plan daring, subversive programmes and recruiting the men to carry them out. This was a seductive world of spies and subterfuge and fearless, almost Bond-like men who would use any means necessary to defeat the enemy. His older brother, now Captain Peter Fleming, served in Norway, Greece and Southeast Asia. He helped create the GHQ Auxiliary Units. This was a top-secret operation to train up units of men who would carry out guerrilla warfare in Britain if the country was ever invaded.

At the start of the war, Peter found time to write a novel in which Adolf Hitler travelled to Britain to negotiate a peace. It would prove remarkably prescient when Hitler's deputy, Rudolph Hess, made a similar journey to England in 1941. Their younger brother, Michael, however, met a tragic end. In October of 1940 he was captured in Normandy, having covered the evacuation, but subsequently died of his wounds.

Ian's contacts in the Ministry of Supply, which was responsible for supplying equipment to British armed forces, would keep him up to date with the gadgets issued to agents in the field, like hollow golf balls for hiding messages, exploding gas pens and shoelaces that doubled as saws. He was part of the team that cooked up one of the war's most daring and successful intelligence deceptions, Operation Mincemeat. A Welsh homeless man, who had died after eating rat poison, was dressed up as a British officer, complete with new identity papers, documents, photos and even love letters from his 'sweetheart'. Also placed in his pockets were invented correspondence between two British generals which suggested the Allies planned to invade Greece and Sardinia. The body, wearing a life jacket, was released from a submarine close to the shore of Spain — apparently the victim of an airplane crash — and was picked up by a Spanish trawler. Franco's Spain was officially neutral, but it was known to the Allies that they provided intelligence to the Nazis. The top secret 'information' found on the corpse was duly passed on to the Germans, causing them to deploy forces away from Sicily, which was the Allies real invasion target.

Towards the end of the war, a friend asked Fleming what he would do when it was all over. He told him his plan was to write the 'spy novel to end all spy novels'. During his service, Fleming had a three-day stopover in Jamaica. 'It was July,' he remembered, 'and brown rain fell in thick rods between periods when everything sweated and steamed. I adored it all.' He vowed to return, and after the war he did just that. He had a simple two-bedroom house built in a secluded cove in the northern region of Oracabessa. He took charge of the design, deciding there would be no glass windows, just customary Jamaican jalousie blinds to let in the air and sun. He named it 'Goldeneye' after the code word for a secret wartime operation.

'Poets and solitaries and crooks love islands,' said Fleming. 'They are for the adventurer rather than the homebody.' When he did finally get around to writing the spy novel he'd been talking about for years, the men he worked with during the conflict would be a rich seam of source material in creating his characters. One figure who would inspire 'M': Admiral John Godfrey, Fleming's superior at the Naval Intelligence Department. He could be terse, moody and difficult but he was less than pleased when identified as inspiration to his former underling. 'He turned me into that unsavoury character,' he complained.

However, writing the Bond novels was still a few years away. What Fleming did immediately after the war was get back into the newspaper business. He took a job as Foreign

Manager for Kemsley Newspapers, which at the time owned the Sunday Times along with other titles. He looked after the company's network of foreign correspondents and stringers, supplying stories and copy from around the globe. As part of his contract, he insisted he be allowed to take a lengthy period off each year to spend at the new retreat he had built in Oracabessa.

Every January he would head out there for a few months. His neighbour was a close friend, the writer and actor Noël Coward. Sometimes for entertainment, Ian would purchase the carcass of a cow or donkey. He would have it pitched into the sea close to his simple abode just so he and his guests could watch the sharks' feeding frenzies. In January 1952, after years of procrastination, Ian Fleming finally sat down at his twenty-year-old portable Royal typewriter in his Jamaican retreat and began writing his first novel.

In creating a new spy hero, Fleming said he wanted 'the dullest name I could find'. He took inspiration from one of his favourite books, 'Birds of the West Indies', by an ornithologist called James Bond. When the fictional spy became a household name, the real James Bond would reach out to the author and the pair would eventually meet. Fleming was entertained by stories about the reaction of officials at airports and hotels around the world on being presented with the British passport of 'James Bond'.

1952 was a year of major change in Fleming's life. The divorce of his long-time lover Ann from her second husband, the newspaper baron Lord Rothermere, was finalised. Ann was already pregnant with Fleming's son Caspar, and they were now free to marry. Fleming would later give his reason for writing that first novel as 'the shock of getting married at the age of forty-three'.

His personal life had never been conventional. Since his early twenties he'd had conducted multiple affairs with women, sometimes juggling several lovers at a time. Like Bond, Fleming could be charming and affectionate but equally he could, at times, be cold, aloof, and sadistic. One favoured method of wooing a new young woman was to invite her up to his Belgravia apartment, introduce her to his extensive collection of pornography and enjoy the level of her shock.

With Ann he found his soulmate and someone whose approach to life was as dysfunctional as his own. Ann Charteris was a wealthy aristocrat whose troubled childhood had left a permanent mark on her character. When they first met, by a swimming pool in France in 1936, Ann was already married. They began a passionate affair when her first husband was killed during the war. She had wanted to marry Ian years earlier, but Fleming refused. Instead, she married the wealthy and powerful Esmond Harmsworth, 2nd Viscount Rothermere. However, Ian and Ann continued their affair after the wedding and throughout Ann's marriage. It was a liaison punctuated by passion, violence and a shared taste for sadomasochism.

'I long for you even if you whip me because I love being hurt by you and kissed afterwards,' Ann wrote in one of her letters to Fleming. He was equally explicit about his feelings for her in their correspondence: 'I love whipping you and squeezing you and pulling your black hair, and then we are happy together and stick pins into each other and like each other and don't behave too grown-up.' Despite this all-consuming passion, Fleming continued to have his affairs with other women, and he didn't stop with them when the couple were married in 1952. Ann would go on to complain: 'You mention "bad old bachelor days" — the only person you stopped sleeping with when they ceased was me.'

Ian and Ann had a complex and dysfunctional

relationship: a coupling that could probably only exist in the bedrooms of the British upper classes. Like Fleming's creation, both were spurred on by danger and violence. Fleming's simple home on the island of Jamacia was his refuge, and his escape from the dreary, rainy streets of London in winter. It made sense that it was here that he would finally sit down and create a special British government agent who was a fantasy invention. One who would be more violent, more sexual and more amoral in defiance of the traditions of British fictional heroes.

According to Fleming: 'Bond's detached; he's disengaged. But he's a believable man, around whom I try to weave a great web of excitement and fantasy. In that, at least, we have very little in common.' However, he did share with his hero many of his own tastes and habits: both men preferred to wear short sleeves shirts and eat scrambled eggs. Both men chain-smoked and drank heavily. Like Fleming, Bond came with a backstory of public school and wartime intelligence work. Like the author, he enjoyed sports cars, gambling, and a parade of beautiful women.

Fleming would push back on suggestions the character was based on him but seemed to enjoy it when reporters made assumptions blurring the line between the character and his creator. He gave Bond many of his other character traits. A certain arrogance and snobbery and a disdain for the 'cradle to grave' welfare state that Labour set about creating in Britain after the war.

Friends of the author said that, at times, Ian Fleming could display a kind of contempt for women and certainly he could behave cruelly towards them. That would be another Bond characteristic. His friend Noël Coward said: 'James Bond was Ian's dream fantasy of what he would like to be, you know, ruthless and dashing.'

In the late 1950s, the British literary scholar and poet

A STRONGLY MARKED STREAK OF VOYEURISM & SADOMASOCHISM

Bernard Bergonzi analysed Fleming's work and concluded the books displayed 'a total lack of any ethical frame of reference'. He also said they contained 'a strongly marked streak of voyeurism and sado-masochism'. He could have been talking about the author.

In *The Spy Who Loved Me*, Fleming puts these words into the mouth of his female narrator: 'All women love semi-rape … It was his sweet brutality against my bruised body that had made the act of love so piercingly wonderful.' In reality, Bond was not Fleming. The character was more a composite of the commandos and officers he had known and served with during the war. A projection of the idolised father who died when he was a child, as well as a certain amount of wish fulfilment for a man who spent most of the war safely behind a desk in London.

Bond was, said Fleming, somewhat dismissively, 'very much a Walter Mitty syndrome, just what you expect from an adolescent mind — which I happen to possess.' One real life inspiration was likely Richard Sorge, a Soviet agent who played a crucial role in the Second World War. Sorge worked undercover as a reporter in Nazi Germany and Japan and was able to inform his Soviet bosses of Germany's planned invasion of Russia, which helped Stalin in his preparations. He also revealed that Japan was not going to invade Russia, which meant Stalin could free up and move battalions across the nation to fight the Nazis. Sorge was eventually arrested, tortured and hung by the Japanese. His espionage activities contributed to saving the Soviet Union and preventing the triumph of the Nazis. Here was a secret agent who actually did save the world. Not for nothing did Fleming say: 'Sorge was the man whom I regard as the most formidable spy in history.'

With his first novel, he established the writing pattern which would help him turn out a Bond book every year until his death. He rose at 7.30am every day and swam naked in his private cove. After breakfast, his favourite meal of the day, he would relax until ten o'clock. Then he started typing. He composed in his head as he wrote, breaking around noon, stopping for lunch, with maybe a quick swim and an afternoon nap. Then back to the typewriter until supper, followed by an evening spent drinking and entertaining friends.

By following that regime, he produced around 2,000 words a day. He would repeat the process every day until he had 70,000 to 80,000 words on the page. He never went back to read over what he had written until the first draft was finished. That was how Fleming pounded out the first draft of *Casino Royale* in just ten weeks.

The way he wrote, and the speed at which he wrote, were crucial for Fleming. He believed it helped create the fast-moving flow of the action and gave the Bond books a sweeping quality. Fleming would refer to the 'puff and zest' he brought to producing his novels. There were lots of rich details, vivid descriptions, along with researched technical information and specifics which gave the stories a stratum of authenticity. The American author, Raymond Benson, who would be one of the small army of writers who would produce new Bond novels after Ian's death, identified what he called 'The Fleming Sweep', ending each chapter which a dramatic hook which pulled the reader into the next chapter.

A few days after finishing that first draft of *Casino Royale*, Ian married Ann in a civil ceremony in Port Maria, Jamaica. Only when he was back in England did he begin the process of revising the copy, adding scenes and correcting his work. What would become familiar elements of the Bond canon were already in place with *Casino Royale*. There were the recurring characters. The stern authority

A STRONGLY MARKED STREAK OF VOYEURISM & SADOMASOCHISM

figure in Bond's life, M, along with a secretary called Miss Moneypenny. The CIA operative called Felix Leiter and James' only friend in the service, and M's chief of staff, Bill Tanner. There were the exotic cocktails and elegant dining, and a beautiful and sexually available companion, who would betray him and come to a bad end. And, with Le Chiffre, there was the first Bond villain: brilliant, psychotic, physically impaired, and a sadist. There was also an astonishing level of sadism in this debut novel. Bond is tied to a chair, his buttocks and genitals exposed, and he is beaten around this area until he passes out from the pain. Alongside that was all the glamour and excitement of the casino and high stakes gambling. There was the exotic, foreign locations and the sex and the violence that his future core audiences, trapped in mundane, suburban lives, will enjoy on their daily commute to their steady, safe office jobs.

But right now, back in London, Fleming was uncharacteristically shy about showing his manuscript to too many people. Finally, he handed a copy to a war time friend, William Plomer, who was a poet but, crucially, also a reader for the publishing house, Jonathan Cape. Ian told him: 'I really am thoroughly ashamed of it. After rifling through this muck, you will probably never speak to me again, but I have got to take that chance.' Plomer did read it and was impressed enough to recommend it up to his publisher bosses.

Jonathan Cape already published the successful travel books of his older brother Peter. Even now, in his forties, it seemed that Ian was still in his older brother's shadow. *Casino Royale* was published in hardcover by Cape on 13 April 1953, priced at 10s, 6d and with a cover designed by Fleming. This was the year of the young Queen's Coronation and Fleming, who would

41

always be looking for any marketing trick to push his book sales, figured a vaguely regal title might help shift a few more copies.

Right from the commencement of his novel writing career, Fleming was consumed with the idea of getting Bond on screen. In a later article on the art of writing a thriller, Fleming confessed that he wrote 'unashamedly for pleasure and money. You don't make a great deal of money from royalties and translation rights and so forth and unless you are very industrious and successful, you could only just about live on these profits, but if you sell the serial rights and film rights, you do very well.' Before the publication of Casino Royale, Fleming wrote to a friend: 'What I want is not a publisher but a "factory" that will shift this opus of mine like, *Gone with the Naked and the Dead*.' Norman Mailer's debut novel, *The Naked and the Dead*, had been an immediate bestseller and was adapted into a film in late fifties. The Oscar laden 1939 film version of Margaret Mitchell's epic novel, *Gone with The Wind*, was the highest grossing picture of its day and would hold that title for a quarter of a century.

Fleming was certainly not lacking in ambition, and he displayed a decidedly un-English honesty about money. 'I am not being vain about this book but simply trying to squeeze every last dirty cent out of it.' While working on final drafts of Casino Royale he splashed out on a rather indulgent present for himself. A gold plated Royal Quiet Deluxe typewriter, purchased at his request by a friend in New York at a cost of $174. Fleming didn't actually write his novels using the appliance, but it was an apt marker of his raging ambition.

Ahead of the publication he bought a small theatrical agency which would primarily be used to act as a corporate body to control the literary copyright of his novels. If the books were a success and there were films that followed it would be a shrewd move to lower his tax bill. Central to his novel was a ruthless British Government agent with 'coldness and a hint of anger in his grey blue eyes'. Effectively this civil servant was an executioner for the Government. He even came with a special 'licence to kill'. Fleming's ambition was that this James Bond fellow would be someone he could turn into the recurring hero of a set of books.

Even from that first outing, Bond was a character conflicted about what he has to do for his country. Toward the end of the novel, he chats with a French intelligence ally, Rene Mathis. 'When one's young, it seems easy to distinguish between right and wrong… At school it's easy to pick out one's own villains and heroes and one grows up wanting to be a hero and kill villains.' Bond then reveals that he was awarded his Double 00 number in the intelligence service for the cold-blooded killing of two men. 'That's all very fine,' says Bond 'The hero kills two villains, but when the hero Le Chiffre starts to kill the villain Bond and the villain Bond knows he isn't a villain at all, you see the other side of the medal. Then villains and heroes all get mixed up.'

Casino Royale was an immediate success with British readers. Its attractions were obvious. Fleming produced exciting, fast-moving stories. They were sexy, violent, edge of the seat adventures set against the backdrop of a recognisable political-economic world as it then was. These were *Boy's Own* stories, with a hook at the end of every chapter, which swept away the cobwebs of the staid, Edwardian adventure novels Fleming grew up reading. As the popularity of the Bond novels spread, Fleming would be alarmed that his stories, which he had intended for an adult audience, would be so popular with schoolboys. He did not want the next generation of young Englishmen to look at James Bond and regard him as a hero or a role model. Bond was to be viewed, in his words, 'only as an efficient professional in his job'. He really shouldn't have been surprised that the work produced by his 'adolescent mind' would appeal to adolescents. Bond's world was an exciting fantasy land of beautiful and available women, with lashings of violence and action and derring-do. What teenage boy would not respond to that?

The books were a heady mix of sex, violence and rampant consumerism. There was all the glamour of high-class casinos and nightclubs, fast cars, exotic locations, jet air-travel, beautifully tailored suits, hand-made shirts, designer watches, individually blended cigarettes, specifically mixed cocktails and the Beretta or the Walther PPK tucked neatly in the underarm holster. In the tired out, black and white world of 1950s Britain, a country of smog, food rationing, and bombed out buildings, Bond was a glorious Technicolor fantasy of previously unimaged luxury, mysterious foreign climes, and unconstrained consumption.

The British general public of 1953 had to get by on spam fritters and tinned fruit. They would have found descriptions of foie gras and salads with thousand islands dressing as exotic and alien as all those foreign countries Bond landed up in. Despite all the fantasy, or maybe because of it, Bond seemed to be the hero the country needed at that time. This was a nation that had won the war but was struggling with how to win, or even navigate, the peace. All of the old certainties were crumbling. Britain was shedding much of its empire, losing out in global status to the new superpowers of America and Russia. This new world order was messy and complex. A grubby place that would soon see Britain's reputation tarnished by duplicitous Cambridge spies and humiliation in the Suez Crisis. Into this confusing arena arrives Bond, a patriot, but a savage and amoral one. A lone assassin, working outside the boundaries of accepted rules and laws and fair play, with a literal license to murder for his country. He emerged out of a time of uncertainty as a fantasy protector, a knight-errant who had clarity and purpose, who could identify the enemy and then destroy him, even if it was all make-believe. It didn't hurt that in this fantasy version of the modern world, Fleming had created one plucky Englishman who would be the only person able to save the world, and America, multiple times.

In *You Only Live Twice*, Fleming gives his character a fiery speech that reflected the author's old-fashioned and deeply conservative views of his rapidly altered nation state: 'Let me tell you this my fine friend, England may have been bled pretty thin by a couple of world wars, our welfare state politics may have made us expect too much for free, and the liberation of our colonies may have gone too fast, but we still climb Everest and beat plenty of the world at plenty of sports and win Nobel Prizes. Our politicians may be a feather-pated bunch, but I expect yours are too. All politicians are. But there's nothing wrong with the British people — although there are only fifty million of them.'

The popular fictional creations of any age do not come into existence in a vacuum. They are always, in some way or another, a reflection of the times they arrive in. If Bond was violent, cruel and sexually promiscuous, it was a reflection of the experiences his creator and his country had gone through. There had just been a war that had claimed the lives of somewhere between 70 million and 85 million people globally. The conflict had decimated a continent and left major European cities in ruins. People around the world had seen the death camps of the Nazis in the cinema newsreels. And if this Bond character was capable of torture and sadism, he was only echoing the real-life activities hidden away in jail cells and interrogation rooms in dark, troubled places like Algeria.

The constant threat of death in the war years had quietly corrupted the public morals. Families had been split apart by military service. The act of living with the fear of bombs dropping and the close proximity of death had all worked to loosen the mores of the civilian population, as much as those in uniform. The nightly air raid sirens, the blackouts and the bunkers under London and the major cities all created opportunities for furtive love making and illicit relationships. Fleming might not have fully recognised it, but this public were hungry for entertainments that spoke to this changing world.

Casino Royale was praised by critics for its fast-moving plot and imaginatively evil villain, but when the novel was published in America it only did modest business. The 'Royale' of the title might have brought him some additional sales in the UK, but it possibly confused potential US readers. *Casino Royale* was eventually reissued In America under the title *Too Hot To Handle*. In 1954, John F Kennedy, who was a senator at the time, was laid up after back surgery and, with time on his hands, read *Casino Royale*. He became a big Bond fan. The last film he would watch at the White House before his assassination in Texas, nearly a decade later, would be *From Russia With Love*. Bizarrely, Lee Harvey Oswald was allegedly reading a Bond novel the night before he fired the fatal shots.

Despite those early positive reviews, there were plenty of readers who were turned off by the cruelty of the central character, and the lack of substance in the women portrayed in the novel. Even some of those close to Fleming had suggested major revisions to *Casino Royale* before publication. Noël Coward, his friend and neighbour in Jamaica, was one of the first to read the book in draft and praised it with patronising condescension. Nearly ten years later Coward would be offered the role of the central villain, Dr No, in the film version of the novel of that name. His written reply: 'Dr No? No! No! No!'

Ann, Fleming's new wife, was not a fan. Nor were Fleming's former girlfriends. They complained that the women in the novel were two-dimensional cardboard cut-outs, only there to sate Bond's sexual appetites. Clare Blanchard, a former lover and part inspiration for the character of Miss Moneypenny, advised him not to publish the book, or at least to do so under a pseudonym. In that first novel, Bond outlined his philosophy regarding the fairer sex: 'Women were for recreation. On a job, they got in the way and fogged things up with sex and hurt feelings and all the emotional baggage they carried. One had to look out for them and take care of them.'

If you were feeling charitable towards the author, you might point out that these females were, at least, independent characters who were not defined by motherhood or marriage, or even the desire for marriage. They wanted to sleep with Bond, or kill him, or both, but very few of them were remotely interested in settling down with him and starting a family. Bond women could usually fend for themselves. They were free spirited and independent, and not reliant on men. They were certainly more independent than the traditional representation of women in the 1950s. It was one of the ways that the Bond of the novels, and, when they arrived, the Bond of the movies, mirrored and foreshadowed the changes in social attitudes and mores coming down the road. Bond and, by extension, these Bond girls, were living the dream life of the liberated swinging sixties, but they were doing it long before the 1960s. Fleming fought back against criticisms of Bond's lifestyle and his excesses. 'You cannot have thrilling heroes eating rice pudding,' he drawled.

With *Casino Royale*, Fleming established a working pattern that would continue for the rest of his days. At the start of every year, he would fly out to Goldeneye and write the first draft of a new Bond novel. When he returned to London, he would work on the redrafts and corrections before handing it across to his publisher. The books quickly gained a large and devoted following and there were critics willing to praise them. Fleming insisted his fictional output was meant as entertainment with no pretensions to literature. But there were signs, especially in the early novels, of an aspiration to be taken seriously as a writer.

For all the glamour and unlikely adventures in exotic places, Fleming had rooted his stories in the real post-war world. An uncertain place of atomic and nuclear energy and competing superpowers. A place where, as Bond complained: 'the heroes and the villains keep on changing parts.' Technological advances now meant it was theoretically possible for unspeakably bad people or movements to bring down governments, carry out seismic global crimes and even destroy the planet.

Fleming admired hard-boiled American pulp fiction authors like Dashiell Hammett and Raymond Chandler. Chandler's hero detective, Philip Marlowe, was another tarnished knight, a cynical anti-hero who wades through the corruption and dark underbelly of LA life, but somehow emerges honourably, doing the noble thing and standing up for the oppressed. Fleming was particularly taken with the writer Mickey Spillane, whose hero Mike Hammer was another streetwise, avenging angel.

One of Fleming's other literary heroes was the English

A STRONGLY MARKED STREAK OF VOYEURISM & SADOMASOCHISM

novelist Graham Greene, another self-proclaimed producer of 'entertainments'. Certainly, Fleming wanted his novels to be classified as spy thrillers rather than as highbrow books. For one thing, thrillers sold more copies than serious literature. However, he aspired to create 'thrillers designed to be read as literature,' which was what Greene had achieved. Greene's 'entertainments' contained compelling stories on themes of moral ambiguity, with complex antagonists battling inner demons. The novels investigated serious issues: totalitarianism, religious persecution, and betrayal — betrayal of lovers, of country, of God, of self. Greene was a serious novelist. And, like Fleming, he had some experience working for the British intelligence services during his many trips abroad. But perhaps the big difference was that in every Greene book there is a character in search of a moral core. Bond, in a myriad of novels and films, is on the hunt for many things, but in none of them is he looking for a moral core.

The two writers were acquainted. Fleming's partner Ann held regular salons at her London apartment. These were gatherings of her acquaintances, drawn from the ranks of intellectuals, artists and writers, and which Greene occasionally attended. Fleming usually hated the meetings, convinced that Ann's highbrow friends were dismissive of his juvenile spy books. Nonetheless, he was eager to get an endorsement from the great man and he offered up his Goldeneye retreat for Greene to stay at, free of charge. The quid pro quo would be that Greene would provide a book jacket endorsement for Fleming's work.

Greene said: 'He agreed to let me have it rent free if I would write an introduction to an omnibus volume of his novels in America, and I had rather tactfully to explain that I would prefer to pay rent.' To make matters worse, Greene would accuse Fleming's beloved housekeeper at Goldeneye, Violet, of overcharging him for alcohol, calling her 'a villainous old housekeeper with the evil eye'. Greene also provided inspiration for Fleming's other great ambition. To see his work make the leap from the page onto the big screen. Greene's novels, including *The Heart of the Matter*, *The End of the Affair*, *Brighton Rock* and *The Power and The Glory* were all given the screen treatment. Filmmakers seemed to be queueing out the door for the opportunity to turn Greene's stories into cinema. Soon after the publication of *Casino Royale*, it looked like Fleming's dream to see Bond translated to the screen would be quickly realised. The American corporation CBS paid Fleming $1,000 for the right to adapt *Casino Royale* for television.

The result, however, was a largely forgotten and haphazard one-hour live drama, with Bond played by Barry Nelson, a jobbing American actor. Nelson had not read the novel — nor had he heard of James Bond — before signing on for the role. His character was now an American agent, called Jimmy Bond, who was working for the 'Combined Intelligence Agency'. Just to further confuse any viewer who might have actually read the novel, the US operative created by Fleming, and called Felix Leiter in the book, was now a British secret agent called Clarence.

Barry Nelson was not proud of his status as the 'first screen Bond'. He said of the film: 'It needed rewriting, more time in rehearsal, a bigger budget. It was done in haste, the exotic flavour of the story was totally lost, and they just dismantled the character.' The live broadcast was full of hiccups and errors. Just prior to filming, the producers estimated that the script was running a few minutes over time, so some quick, last-minute cuts were made to the dialogue, which served to further confuse the narrative.

What it did have was Peter Lorre playing the central

villain, Le Chiffre. If there was ever a character actor who would make a perfect Bond villain, it should have been Lorre, who had perfected many memorably villainous roles in classics like *The Maltese Falcon*. Sadly, the film was a waste of his and everyone else's talents. Audiences watching at home would see Bond murder Le Chiffre and then, before the camera had time to shift away, the dead man getting up from the floor and walking off the set. Bond's debut screen outing impressed no one, least of all Fleming. There would be other attempted film and TV projects, which would excite, energise and then, ultimately, disappoint the writer.

The famed director and producer Alexander Korda was interested in making a film version of *Live and Let Die*, the second Bond novel. The Hungarian born mogul had been a giant of British cinema in the thirties and forties, producing the *Private Life of Henry VIII* and *The Four Feathers* among other epics, but his interest came to nothing. Korda was in ill health and couldn't raise the finances.

The Rank Organisation, then one of the major — and majorly failing — British studios, took an option on *Moonraker* but let it lapse after six months. An eager, young, would-be producer approached Fleming about a television project aimed at boosting the Jamaican tourist industry. Fleming produced a twenty-eight-page outline of stories for the proposed series tentatively called *Commander Jamaica*, or *James Gunn: Secret Agent*. The hero would be a thinly disguised version of James Bond and the series would all be filmed on the island. The series was duly optioned and then promptly went nowhere. When the rights returned to him, Fleming incorporated some the script ideas into his sixth Bond novel, *Dr No*.

He had entered into a relationship with the *Daily Express* in Britain which ran serialisations of some of his books and a cartoon serial of the Bond stories which became enormously popular. All the same, it wasn't cinema. A film producer and actor called Gregory Ratoff offered $6,000 for the film rights of *Casino Royale* in perpetuity. And Fleming, needing the money, accepted. Ratoff died before he ever did anything with the rights.   An American producer working out of London had been an early fan of the novels and made an offer for the rights to Ratoff's widow. She turned him down, selling it instead to a Hollywood lawyer, agent and producer Charles K Feldman.

Even without Greene's stamp of approval, Fleming did have a growing base of American fans. Raymond Chandler had been one of Fleming's favourite writers and a source of inspiration. Chandler returned the compliment, praising *Live and Let Die*, saying: 'It is probably the most forceful and driving of what I suppose still must be called thrillers in England.' Nonetheless, by the late 1950s, the monotony of producing a new Bond adventure every year was starting to grate on its author. Fleming was appreciative of the financial success of the novels, but he was beginning to despise the creature he had created. It was increasingly hard work trying to come up with new perils and fresh adventures for the agent, as well as invent unique super villains and new ways for his hero to save the world and save himself. Astute critics noticed that the quality of the stories and the writing was noticeably declining. He still had his loyal following, but more discerning readers were registering Fleming's boredom with his creation.

In 1956 Fleming was invited by a friend to join a scientific expedition to a flamingo colony on the island of Inagua in the Bahamas. The team had to rough it in tents and Fleming was able to utilise the experience in his next Bond novel, *Dr No*. In the book, the island would become the model for *Dr No*'s Crab Key and the marsh buggy they drove around in inspired the 'dragon tank', which the Dr would use to scare away inquisitive visitors. The central story of *Dr No* had been inspired by real events. Failed early rocket tests had put the US behind the Russians in the Space Race and there was deep political unrest in the Caribbean. In the novel, Fleming set out the shifting plates of a fading British influence in the region. It opens at the elite Queens Club, a white pilloried establishment with wide lawns and tennis courts, '...the social mecca of Kingston. Such stubborn retreats will not long survive in modern Jamaica', wrote Fleming. 'One day Queens Club will have its windows smashed and perhaps be burned to the ground, but for the time being it was a useful place to find in a sub-tropical island — well run, well-staffed and with the finest cuisine and cellar in the Caribbean.'

When *Dr No* was published in 1958, Ian Fleming received some of his harshest reviews. Journalist Paul Johnson, writing in the *New Statesman*, was savage. *Dr No*, he said, was 'the nastiest book I have ever read. By the time I was a third of the way through, I had to suppress my strong impulse to throw the thing away, and only continued reading because I released that here was a social phenomenon of some importance — Fleming deliberately and systematically excites, and then satisfies the very worst instincts of his readers.' Johnson said the key ingredients of a Bond story were: 'The sadism of a schoolboy bully, the mechanical two-dimensional sex-longings of a frustrated adolescent, and the crude snob-cravings of a suburban adult.' Other reviewers noted that this was perhaps the weakest of the Bond books so far. The lousy reviews did nothing to affect sales, with *Dr No* outselling its predecessors.

A childhood friend of Fleming's, Ivar Bryce, suggested to the writer that they produce a Bond film themselves, not adapted from any of the books but with entirely new material. They hired a young, ambitious Irish filmmaker, Kevin McCrory, who, with another writer and with contributions from Fleming, produced a working script. Bryce and McClory had already worked together on a low-budget film, *The Boy and the Bridge*, which Fleming saw in rough cut and enjoyed very much.

Their new project, tentatively called *Latitude 78 West*, involved the hijacking of atomic bombs from a jet plane. The storyline included a sinister, global criminal organisation — SPECTRE — which stood for Special Executive for Counterintelligence, Terrorism, Revenge and Extortion, and was headed by the villainous Ernst Stavro Blofeld. When the film project, inevitably, fell through, Fleming went back to his typewriter and plotted out his next Bond novel, to be called *Thunderball*. He used key elements of the screenplay as a basis for the story. It was an editorial decision that would give the world two of Bond's most memorable and enduring foes, SPECTRE and Blofeld. However, it would also land the author into a long, exhausting, and costly legal battle.

CBS again came calling. What about a possible TV series based around a British Bond? At least this time they didn't want to change the agent's nationality. Fleming was concerned about how Americans. and particularly American producers, seemed to view the English. He produced a memo outlining how he thought his hero should be developed for the US small screen. What he wanted to avoid, at all costs, was 'too much stage Englishness. There should, I think, be no monocles, moustaches, bowler hats, bobbies or other 'limey' gimmicks. There should be no blatant English slang, a minimum of public-school ties and accents, and subsidiary characters should generally speak with a Scots or Irish accent. The Secret Service should be presented as a tough, modern organisation.' The proposal was another project that failed to launch.

There was a meeting arranged with a couple of American film producers working out of London, at Les Ambassadeurs Club in Mayfair, buy only one of the producers actually turned up at the appointed time. The other, Cubby Broccoli, was a fan of the books but he had flown to New York to look after his terminally ill wife. Cubby's partner, Irving Allen, was definitely not in the Bond fan club. He practically insulted Fleming and his work, saying it wasn't even good enough for TV, and walked out. By the end of the decade, it was even more obvious to friends and to many fans of the novels that Fleming had grown sick and tired of his creation. To keep himself amused, he developed a mischievous fondness for using the names of friends and acquaintances for characters in his novels. He took particular pleasure in applying real people's names for his villains.

An architect by the name of Erno Goldfinger went to his lawyers and threatened to halt publication of the 1959 Bond novel which used his surname as its title and principal baddie. This real Goldfinger had a reputation for being utterly humorous and had reportedly sacked staff for being inappropriately jocular. Fleming's characteristic response was to write to his publishers suggesting they 'change the name to Goldprick and provide an explanation of the reason why'.

The publishers did not take his advice. In the end Erno did not sue. The publishers paid his solicitor costs and gave him six free copies of the book. It was another bestseller, although it was also pilloried by the critics. Even those who praised *Casino Royal* were turning against Fleming, complaining about lazy plotting and increasingly absurd baddies.

A review from *The Tatler* said: 'It is getting harder and harder to know what on earth to make of Mr Bond. With *Goldfinger*, his creator, Mr Ian Fleming, seems to me to be getting as close to self-parody as to make no difference and even to a once devoted Bond admirer such as myself, the old familiar mixture of preposterous plot, fantasy, cruelty, and "blind them with science" technical talk, no longer seems quite such a lark as before. One might guess that Mr Fleming is possibly beginning just faintly to despise his own puppets, and the market for them.'

Meanwhile Fleming was toying with the notion of killing off Bond. Although, even as he grew to loathe creation, he still enjoyed the income and celebrity the novels provided, but resented the time he had to spend telling his stories. In *The Spy Who Loved Me*, which was published in 1962, Bond doesn't turn up until two thirds of the way through the book. His public punished Fleming by making it the worst seller in the series.

Fleming was growing equally cynical about these people from the film industry who came knocking with big promises, which they then failed to deliver on. One person who had been impressed by *Goldfinger* was a Canadian producer operating in London, named Harry Saltzman. He read the book and figured this Bond character might be perfect material for the screen. In December 1960, Fleming was invited to yet another meeting with an overseas film producer based in London. He soon found himself back at the same venue where he had been insulted by Irving Allen: Les Ambassadeurs Club. After nearly a decade of near misses, stalled projects and options falling through, he can't have held out much hope that this Saltzman character was going to be any different. Nonetheless, scepticism did not stop Fleming accepting $50,000 of Saltzman's money

A STRONGLY MARKED STREAK OF VOYEURISM & SADOMASOCHISM

for six-months' rights to the majority of his novels.

Fleming himself almost scuppered the deal before it was signed. Sometime earlier he had been at lunch with a glamourous American actress turned producer, Ann Marlow. In a spontaneous decision, Fleming signed away, on a napkin, the television rights of his novels to his beautiful dining companion. Apparently, it didn't seem to have occurred to him that the film producer giving him $50,000 for the options rights could possibly mind that his proposed films would likely face competition from a rival television Bond. Fleming had to contact the producer and backtrack on his impetuous arrangement and, luckily for him, Marlow did not play hardball.

As soon as *Thunderball* was published in 1961, Fleming ran into further legal troubles. He had made no mention or acknowledgement of the screen writer Kevin McCrory, or the other writer, in his novel, or to their contribution to the storyline. The pair were heading to court claiming rights over the story and it would be the start of a long, protracted and stressful legal battle with the author.

Fleming had a heart attack days after the legal action started. While he lay in a hospital bed recuperating, he got a get-well message from Harry Saltzman and his new business partner Cubby Broccoli, along with a note detailing their fresh new deal with an American film studio, United Artists, to make a Bond movie. The producers had been thinking that Fleming's latest, *Thunderball*, would make a good first film. They already had a screenwriter working up a draft script. That plan would have to be hastily abandoned with these legal troubles.

But now, in 1962, here they all were, in Jamaica. They were actually filming scenes that Fleming had put to paper. A real-life Bond film was actually being made. Fleming's big dream was becoming a reality. There had been no shortage of failed movie deals and aborted option rights. A lengthy roll call of studios and directors and writers and producers who all promised to translate Bond into celluloid or onto television, and virtually every one of those deals had fallen through. And the one that made it, the American TV drama based on his first book, was easily and best forgotten, especially by anyone who saw it broadcast. On the other hand, Fleming had the satisfaction — and an all-important bump in books sales — of President John F Kennedy including his novel *From Russia with Love* on a list of favourite books.

Fleming was not yet convinced the north American producers knew what they were doing. He still suspected the 'unrefined' working class Scottish actor they employed to play Bond was a serious piece of miscasting. In some of the previous screen attempts, Ian had himself tried his hand at scriptwriting, but this time he left the producers to it. In the early drafts of the *Dr No* script, the writers had shifted away from the story in the novel. A long way away.

The Dr Julius No of the book was a Chinese German who had hooks for hands after his own were cut off by Tong gangsters. In their embryonic script, he had, for some inexplicable reason, been turned into a monkey. Broccoli and Saltzman had sent the script back to the writers and *Dr No* was given back his original back story, but with the hooks replaced by metal prosthetic hands. It was now a full decade since Fleming sat down to write *Casino Royale*, the first of his novels about 'an anonymous blunt instrument wielded by a government department'.

Achieving his long-held desire to see Bond up on a big screen came at a difficult part in his life. His health was deteriorating. His alcoholism and the life-long, chain-smoking were catching up on him. Despite suffering the heart attack, he was still ignoring doctors' advice. He now had a new, pressing reason for hoping this latest Bond film would take off. He wanted to ensure his wife Ann and son Caspar were well looked after when he died. Producing a series of best-selling novels on both sides of the Atlantic was all very well, but Ann was a woman of expensive tastes, and Fleming always knew the big money was in films.

Maybe these two north American chaps could defy his pessimism and produce a movie that would live up to Fleming's considerable ambitions and would help ensure the future comfort of his family.

Ian Fleming was the third husband of the socialite,
Ann Charteris. They had an unconventional marriage
and a shared taste for sadomasochism.

3 All I'm out for is a good time; the rest is propaganda

arry Saltzman tried his hand at many occupations on the long road to becoming a film producer. One of the earliest was selling soap out of the back of a truck. He would pull up in a small town and pretend one of the wheels on his wagon needed to be changed. He stripped off his shirt, set about fixing it and, in the process, covered himself in black axle grease. Then, as the assembled crowd watched with astonishment, he'd wash the grease off his body with miraculous ease, using his special soap. It was a scam of course. The axle grease was really black soap. But already, here was a young man who knew how to put on a show for the punters.

British director and screenwriter Ken Hughes, who worked with Saltzman on several films, said: 'Only a Harry Saltzman could have made a Bond picture. He's a modern-day Barnum.' Herschel Saltzman was born in 1915 in Sherbrooke, a city in Quebec, Canada, to a Jewish immigrant father from Poland. He had his first taste of showbusiness when the family moved to Cleveland, Ohio, where he got an after-school job sweeping up in a Vaudeville theatre.

ALL I'M OUT FOR IS A GOOD TIME; THE REST IS PROPAGANDA

His wasn't a happy childhood. His mother died young, he was beaten by his father and persecuted by teachers for the perceived moral defect of being left-handed. He left home at 15, actually running off and joining a travelling circus. By the early 1930s he had relocated to Paris, originally to study politics and economics, but he started working as a talent scout, supplying performers to music halls and circuses across Europe. Harry travelled around the continent seeking out and booking the best acts, often in fierce competition with other booking agents. Along the way he acquired a good command of German and Spanish to go with his French.

It was 1938, and the storm clouds of war were gathering. His Paris agency had two million marks deposited in banks in Berlin which the fascist German government refused to allow to be taken out of the country. Harry volunteered to travel to Germany in an attempt to free up the funds, a reckless proposition given his Jewish heritage. While he couldn't take the money out of the country, he could access the funds to buy train tickets and ship passages to transport acrobats, circus acts and theatre performers safely out of Nazi Germany, whittling away the deposits held in the banks. He used some of the money to bribe Nazi officials to allow the unhampered passage of Jewish performers.

Harry finally got himself out of the country after a warning visit to his hotel from police officers and then a tip off from a Gestapo connected theatre manager that he was attracting unwanted attention. When war broke out Saltzman went home and signed up for the Royal Canadian Air Force in Vancouver. His military career then took a fascinating turn that might have a bearing on his future status as a producer of spy movies.

After being discharged from the Canadian Air Force,

he joined the psychological warfare division Office of Strategic Services (OSS) in the States, the predecessor of the CIA. Harry was now back in Europe and north Africa doing work that is still shrouded in mystery. Simon Raven, a friend and writer who worked on the script of *On Her Majesty's Secret Service*, said: 'He was a field officer as we would say in England, I think he was something to do with intelligence.'

Harry's language skills and his first-hand knowledge from travelling around Europe in his previous employment would have been valuable tools for the agency. In 1944, he was in London working out of the US embassy. His principal job was organising the distribution of motion pictures, but it is highly likely he was involved in some form of intelligence work. Even his family were not sure about his war record. His son Steven said: 'He worked definitely for OSS, and he had a role that was never fully described to me but made him work in a clandestine capacity.' There is even speculation that he and Ian Fleming might have crossed paths. The US and British intelligence services were working closely together and here were two men engaged in intelligence duties in the same city. What is likely is that when, years later, he picked up and read a James Bond novel, he would have a personal connection into the wartime secret intelligence world that had inspired and informed Fleming's fictional hero.

After the war, Harry stayed on in Europe, helping set up a film division for UNESCO, designed to spread the gospel of peace and democracy. But he quickly grew disillusioned with the assignment and quit. While living in Paris, he met and married Jacqueline Colin, a refugee from Romania. He would spend the next few years involved in multiple businesses, commuting between America and Europe. One venture involved hiring out coin-operated wooden horses to carnivals. A brief sojourn into the world of advertising didn't work out for him, but he got a job as production manager on a TV series in the States, which proved to be a better fit. It would also provide a solid base for setting himself up in the career that would define him.

In the post war years, American film studios were not allowed to take the profits made showing their films in European cinemas out of the continent. To put the money to good use, they looked at financing films in Europe that could then hopefully make them money with audiences back home in the States. At the same time, in Britain, the Government introduced the Eady Levy, a tax on cinema tickets which would go into a pot of money for use in financing films that used British film technicians and British actors.

The US government had also developed a scheme whereby US citizens who worked abroad for at least 510 days during a period of 18 months would not be taxed on their earnings. The scheme was aimed primarily at American humanitarian workers helping in the rebuilding of the European countries decimated by the war. However, canny agents and producers in Hollywood soon figured out that scriptwriters, actors and directors could also be eligible for the tax breaks if they headed to Europe as part of their employment. For an ambitious would-be producer, there were deals to be had making film and television product in Europe that would attract US financing and studios and exploit the available incentives.

Saltzman, now with television production experience, was not the only north American who spotted the benefits of setting up as a film producer in the bombed-out ruins of Europe. Around the same time, another pair of producers was moving to London to make movies. A tough, seasoned producer and director, Irving Allen along with his new businesses partner, Cubby Broccoli.

Saltzman's first move into producing was a TV series for the NBC network back in America. Hollywood had, over the decades, developed a fascination for the French Foreign Legion, from action dramas like *Beau Geste* and *Under Two Flags* to comic takes from Laurel and Hardy and Abbot and Costello. Harry's television series, *Captain Gallant of the Foreign Legion*, related the highly unlikely exploits of an American expatriate who joins the legion, operating in north Africa. It starred Olympic swimmer turned actor Buster Crabbe, best known for his roles in cowboy B Movies. And the series pretty much played like a cowboy serial, with the addition of a lot of sand. Captain Gallant even had a cowboy style sidekick played by another veteran of the western flicks, Fuzzy Knight. Saltzman convinced Crabbe to sign up for the production by throwing in a supporting role for his son, who was just starting out on a fledging acting career. What made Gallant unusual for American television was that it was shot outside the US, in Morocco and Italy. The series would run for 48 episodes.

Next, the ambitious producer made a bold stride into film, convincing one of the biggest names in American screenwriting to join forces with him. Ben Hecht, a former journalist, was one of the great screenwriters of the Hollywood Golden Age, working on *Angels over Broadway* and *The Front Page* and having a hand in scripting a dozen classic films. When he was contributing to the script for the seminal gangster film, the original *Scarface*, Hecht was visited by a couple of hoods sent by Al Capone, who was concerned that the film was based on his life. Hecht had been a reporter in Chicago and was not unfamiliar with gangsters. He managed to convince the pair that the film was not based on their boss but a composite of serval different people, and they left him alone to get on with his script.

With their new company, named Benhar, the deal was that Hecht would write the screenplays and Harry would take care of the production side of things. Unfortunately, their first production, *The Iron Petticoat*, would turn out to be a disaster, and their last film together. Hecht wrote the screenplay, a cold war comedy, as a vehicle for Katherine Hepburn, with a storyline that owed more than a passing acquaintance to Greta Garbo's pre-war film, *Ninotchka*. Hepburn played a Soviet pilot who lands in Western Europe, falls in love with an American soldier and is seduced by Capitalism. Saltzman and Hecht had hoped to attract Cary Grant or James Stewart to play Hepburn's romantic lead, hopefully recreating some of the magic of the previous films she made with them, like *The Philadelphia Story*. Somehow, they went from Cary Grant and James Stewart to screen comic Bob Hope. Hope was actually born in England, and this would be the comedian's first film made back in the land of his birth. A former lover of Hope had just published an embarrassing tell all-book in the States, tarnishing his wholesome, family man image. Removing himself from the US for a few months might have seemed like a wise public relations move. Unfortunately for the production, Hope arrived in London with his own team of gag writers and proceeded to dismantle Hecht's script, cutting Hepburn's lines substantially and inserting more of his trademark wisecracks.

Saltzman was an extrovert, larger than life man, and one who could be hot headed and downright rude, but he appeared to be no match for Hope. The production was riven with animosity and Hecht ended up asking for his name to be taken off the credits. On its release in the States, he took out a full-page advert in *The Hollywood Reporter* attacking Hope and the damage he had done to the film. It was the most critically reviled films of either stars' career. The critic at the *New York Times* said: 'If this was meant to be a travesty, it has succeeded.' *The Iron Petticoat* did modestly at the US box office but then disappeared for decades, allegedly because Hope blocked it being shown after its initial release. It would not be shown on US television until 46 years later, after the comedian's death. Harry's career as a movie producer had not got off to the best start and his partnership with Hecht didn't last.

Hecht had based himself in the London offices of the Famous Artists Agency. When the agency's representative left for another job, he rented the offices to Harry, and, as part of the deal, the services of his secretary, a young Irish woman — ambitious to break into screenwriting — named Johanna Harwood. 'Harry didn't have a lot of social polish,' remembered Harwood, 'and he was very tactless. That was his main problem, really. He rubbed people up the wrong way very easily. I always used to think he must have looked exactly like he looked in the pram. Which helped him because he looked as if you could trust him, and of course you couldn't, not really.'

Harry started looking around for his next film project. He was an avid theatregoer and became very excited about a radical new 'writers theatre' that had been set up in Chelsea, a few miles from the capital's theatre district. The subsidised English Stage Company, based at the Royal Court Theatre at the top of the King's Road, was set up with an ambitious goal. The company wanted to find and produce the work of a new generation of writers, directors and actors who would re-energise a British theatre that had become staid and out of touch with modern audiences. The company put an ad in *The Stage* newspaper asking for plays and got 700 replies. Among the slush pile, one play, by a struggling young actor named John Osborne, stood out. The company's first production in 1956 was Osborne's *Look Back in Anger*. It was directed by Tony Richardson and did exactly what the company promised. The play's raw language and portrayal of a twisted, cruel marriage between a disaffected working-class husband and his put-upon, middle-class wife outraged and electrified audiences in equal measure. That play, and the Royal Court's subsequent productions, spoke to the anger and frustrations of a new generation, and the seismic shifts occurring in British society. The country was still deep in debt from the Second World War and many London streets were scarred with bombed out buildings from the Luftwaffe attacks, Food rationing only ended in 1954 and Britain's once assured status as a leading world power was sliding away, along with its Empire and influence.

Just a few weeks after the play opened, the Egyptian President, Gamal Abdel Nasser, announced the nationalisation of the Suez Canal Company, a joint British-French concern which had owned the canal since its construction in the 19th century. A cynical British-led ploy to come up with an excuse to invade Egypt had to be abandoned because America, the new global power, refused to back its traditional ally. Britain, the fading Empire nation which for so long had been able to dominate and dictate other nation's affairs, was humiliated on the world stage.

And for many in this new generation of its citizens, the country's corrupt attempts to bully and undermine another nation's independence was symptomatic of a rotten, outdated establishment that needed to be attacked and replaced. Osborne's play was part of a wider explosion of new work in the theatre. Many of these emerging talents did not come from traditional 'posh' theatrical backgrounds, and they certainly didn't want to produce plays like those of the past. They were determined to drag British theatre out of the genteel sitting rooms of Noël Coward and Terrence Rattigan and place it in the kitchen, where real people lived their real lives. A disapproving public relations woman at the Royal Court had labelled Osborne 'an angry young man'. She'd likely meant it as a rebuke, but the moniker would serve as a signpost for this wave of new playwrights and authors. And one of those sitting in the audience at the Royal Court, transfixed by this new school of theatre, was Harry Saltzman.

Alongside the new breed of writers were a fresh generation of actors; Richard Burton, Peter O'Toole, Richard Harris and *Look Back in Anger*'s lead players, Kenneth Haigh and Alan Bates. Here were raw talents that refused to act or speak like traditional English leading men. These were earthy, physical performers, defiantly sexual, arrogant in their talent and their rejection of the well-spoken, reserved performers that had dominated British theatre and films in the 1950s. From the stalls, Saltzman recognised that a powerful new cultural force was being born. It was a theatrical movement that was, in its own way, as revolutionary as the rock 'n' roll that now dominated the social lives of the younger generation. Saltzman was convinced that these new dramatic voices could, with the right handling, become lucrative and global in a similar way to those new sound-makers.

He invited Osborne for tea at the Dorchester and started his charm offensive, courting both Osborne and Richardson by taking them to the finest restaurants, flying them to New York and, always, talking about the creation of a 'writers film company' to match their writers' theatre. He convinced them that *Look Back in Anger* should transfer to New York's Broadway where it opened to triumphant reviews and ran for a year.

Richardson said of Saltzman: 'He had a perfect mogul's figure, stocky, tubby, crinkly grey hair and the face of an eager, coarse cherub. He bubbled with plans and had great charm. He was a splendid raconteur. By his generosity — in big and small things, he always loved to give —he radiated affluence.' The charm offensive worked. The three men formed Woodfall Films, named after the Chelsea street where Osborne lived with his then girlfriend Mary Ure, who also happened to be the lead actress in *Look Back in Anger*.

In an essay, Saltzman laid out the philosophy behind the production company: 'We did not form Woodfall productions from an arty-crafty point of view. We are extremely commercial minded, and we regard the properties we have as commercial properties. But the most important thing about our company is that we insist on having artistic control of our pictures. We want to make them honestly. In other words, we control the scripts, the cast, the shooting, and the completion of the picture. We won't allow our distributors or the people who back us to tell us how to make a picture. It's a hard road, we're the only people doing this in England, and it is a battle all the time.'

After the original backers, Rank, pulled out, Saltzman managed to persuade Warner Brothers to finance, along with Associated British Pathé, their first production, a low-budget adaptation of *Look Back in Anger*. Richardson had never made a film before, but Saltzman, true to his manifesto, fought to have him direct the film version, against opposition from the backers. The £250,000 budget was modest, but this was not a film with location shooting in foreign parts or expensive action sequences. What was most important to Harry was that they would be left alone to make the film that the writer and director wanted to make.

The Welsh actor, Richard Burton, was already an established screen star and at 30, probably a bit too old for the central role of Jimmy Porter. But he was so eager to take over in the lead he agreed to a cut from his usual fee. Harry had high hopes that the film, especially with a recognised name like Burton, would find an eager international audience. After all, the stage play had transferred to Broadway with great success.

First, they had a battle with the British film censor who objected to some of the language translated from the stage play to the script: words like 'virgin', 'bitch' and 'bastard' as well as the lead character Porter's cruel and sadistic tormenting of his wife. Harry and his creative partners held firm on the language and content. Unfortunately, the censor was not going to be swayed either. When the film was released, it was as an adult only feature, greatly reducing its potential audience.

The film attracted critical praise but went on to be a commercial failure, both in the UK and abroad. It was nominated for four Baftas but won none. Harry had arranged a screening of *Look Back in Anger* in Hollywood for Jack Warner, who, after all, had financed the project, About eight minutes into the showing, Warner asked: 'What language are they talking?' Saltzman replied it was English. 'This is America,' said Warner, and he promptly stood up and walked out of the screening room. As Saltzman would say later: 'I never made a film that got such good reviews and was seen by so few people.' He thought the mistake had been the casting of Burton. He learned the hard way how crucial casting could be in a film.

The next film from their production company was another adaption of an Osborne stage play. *The Entertainer*

ALL I'M OUT FOR IS A GOOD TIME; THE REST IS PROPAGANDA

was a savage allegory about Britain's terminal decline using the metaphor of a failing, end of pier comedian, but not even the presence of Sir Laurence Olivier in the lead role of Archie Rice could help it at the box office.

Saltzman was getting disillusioned with Woodfall. He was already moving on from the company just as it released its third production. *Saturday Night and Sunday Morning* was an adaptation of a ground-breaking first novel from another angry young man, Alan Sillitoe. The film was made on a shoestring, with Richardson deferring his producer fee. It went on to be a surprise box office success in Britain and is now regarded as one of the finest British films ever produced. It made an overnight star of its lead, Albert Finney, who played the rebellious, hard living and cynical factory worker in a bleak, working class Nottingham.

The films of Woodfall, and a handful of other filmmakers and writers at the time, established a powerful and influential British New Wave of cinema, which was unafraid to examine and portray working class life in all its brutal honesty. If that had been Saltzman's sole contribution to British cinema, it would have been impressive.

Following the success of Saturday Night and Sunday Morning, Woodfall would continue to make films for the rest of the 1960s, but without Harry's involvement. However, the financial success of *Saturday Night and Sunday Morning* would assist the ever-restless Canadian producer as he set off on his next big cinematic adventure. When Osborne asked Harry what he planned to do after he removed himself from Woodfall, he told him excitedly: 'I bought the Bond books. All of them.'

Saltzman had picked up and read a Bond novel in 1959 and was immediately drawn to this character who was unlike any of the traditional British fictional heroes. Here was a flesh and blood male, a man who could be cruel and stylish but, in the same moment, a man who dominated women and had this strange licence to kill. Bond was not some gentlemen detective or amateur adventurer but a secret service agent, no, more a weapon, of the state. Perhaps Saltzman recognised that Bond, in its own peculiar way, was as much a reaction to Britain's fading global status, as the work of Osborne, Sillitoe and their tribe.

But while the angry young men wanted to attack and dismantle the failing old guard, Fleming's hero could be viewed as a wish fulfilment fantasy for the return of power for that fading Britain. These stories were a dreamland where a single British operative — one who was a product of Eton, where the ruling class sends its offspring — is the only person capable of saving America's bacon, rescuing the world from the brink of destruction, and getting the girl.

Perhaps it took an outsider living in Britain, a migrant removed from the English class system, to identify that Bond represented something that defied how Britain saw itself, and how the rest of humanity saw the nation. Saltzman had tried to sell the world a new version of Britain as portrayed by Osborne. One that was unvarnished, coarse, grim, a black and white reality, and he'd found it a tough sell. Now, with a new decade starting, maybe he'd have better luck convincing the world of this other revision of the nation. A version that was stylish, exotic, sexy, amoral, fantastic and in glorious Technicolor.

When Saltzman started his enquiries regarding the rights to the novel, he discovered that he and Fleming shared the services of the same London solicitor. Brian Lewis was able to set up a meeting between the two men. Before the meeting, Lewis advised Fleming that he ought to seal the film rights sooner rather than later. Fleming was already a very unwell man. His excessive drinking and smoking were catching up with him. The writer was eager to ensure he provided for his family after his death. If he passed away without any new film option, any future deals would be skewed at a low rate, based on the sale of all the rights to *Casino Royale* to Gregory Ratoff for $6,000.

The two men met at Les Ambassadeurs, the exclusive club and casino in Mayfair. Fleming had been convinced Bond would be perfect for the big screen since he sat down to write *Casino Royale* almost ten years earlier. It had been a frustrating decade of endless meetings and option agreements and contracts with a rolling cast of directors, producers and TV and film companies and Ian was jaded from the whole disappointing experience.

Only a few years before, he'd been invited to a similar meeting at the same Les Ambassadeurs, with yet another north American producer based in London. That one had ended prematurely with the producer insulting him and his work, saying James Bond was not even good enough for television. Fleming had plenty of reasons not to get his hopes raised with this latest would-be mogul.

The meeting did not start well. Fleming, displaying more than his usual degree of arrogance and condescension, confessed that the last film he had seen was *Gone With The Wind*, the David O Selznick epic that was released in 1939. Furthermore, he informed Harry Saltzman that he considered film a low form of art. Saltzman could be arrogant and surly himself but, when it was needed, he could also be charming and generous. He responded by setting up a special screening of *Saturday Night and Sunday Morning* for the writer. Fleming attended and was gracious enough to admit to being impressed by the film.

Hilary Saltzman, Harry's daughter, said after his death: 'I've heard the rumours that his and Ian Fleming's paths crossed during the war. Even though they couldn't acknowledge that they had known each other, because then they would be acknowledging what they had done during the war. I think that's a large part of why Ian felt he could trust my father with bringing Bond to the screen. He felt he could trust him with getting across what he wanted Bond to be.'

Saltzman laid out his proposed deal. It would be $50,000 for the six-month option to the Bond catalogue. This was all the books, apart from *Casino Royale*. As part of the deal, Saltzman would agree to pay Fleming an additional $100,000 per Bond film that got made as well as a percentage of net profits. It was a coup for Fleming and a huge financial gamble for Saltzman. Crucially, part of the deal was that if the Bond series became so successful that it exhausted all published work, Saltzman would have the right to make original Bond movies from stories not created by Fleming. Saltzman was now well on his journey away from the production of bleak, grimly realistic kitchen sink dramas and, hopefully, heading towards the sunny climes of bold, expansive, sexy, glamourous fantasy thrillers.

Osborne and his cohorts were producing stories that attempted to show how ordinary people really lived their lives: their stunted ambitions, their failed relationships, their battles for identity and meaning, and their desire to escape the everyday and the mundane. Saltzman was now turning his attention to a world that wasn't about how people lived, but how they wanted to live: a heady fantasy of exotic locations, fast cars. sexually available women along with danger and high living.

Saltzman caught something of the mood of 1950s England with his relationship with, and the output of, the Royal Court crowd. The England of that decade was black and white, and usually grey, London was still a partial bomb site, and frequently smog bound as regulations to control factory pollution had yet to be introduced. Its people were coming to terms with the fact that winning a world war did not solve all problems.

A new generation was coming of age. They were surly and tired of constantly hearing about war time sacrifices, ambitious to reach out and explore better, more exciting lives. They were energised by rock 'n' roll and American movies, and open to the new ideas coming at them off the screen. The country was about to experience a seismic shift in the accepted patterns of social status and societal norms. There were a new generation of people born working class who were not so accepting of their lowly place in the hierarchy,

Saltzman, the outsider, the émigré, recognised something was occurring and he saw a potential goldmine in attempting to bottle some of that energy and those aspirations and presenting them to the world on the screen. The films he made with Osborne and Richardson detailed that anger and frustrated desire for change, any change. It hadn't quite worked out commercially, but at least the films were recognised as quality products.

Now, instead of films that told cinema audiences just how miserable their lives were, he would be making movies that showed them the life that they secretly dreamed off. Saltzman said: 'What people wanted after the kitchen sink, I felt, was something different: strong plots with excitement, fast cars, bizarre situations, drink and women.'

Bond fitted the bill perfectly. His tales detailed everything that was denied to ordinary British people post-war; the jet travel; the impeccably tailored suits; the detailed menus of high-class restaurants; the exotic cocktails mixed in exclusive clubs. The Bond stories had been. and would continue to be, attacked for the treatment and portrayal of women. It was the same reaction of Fleming's girlfriends who were among the first to read *Casino Royale* back in its manuscript form.

The girls were just there for sex, they complained, they were cardboard cut outs, two dimensional characters at best. It was valid criticism, but there was also an argument that there was something quietly revolutionary about the Bond girls as well. Too many female roles in films of the 1950s were also two dimensional. They were the wife, or the girlfriend, or mother, adjuncts of 'important' central male characters.

Even the women in progressive dramas like *Look Back in Anger* and *Saturday Night and Sunday Morning* are defined by their men, usually put-upon girlfriends, neglected wives, nagging mothers. Bond girls were not wife material, as a rule. Only rarely did they want to go steady or marry him. It was a way that Fleming and his invented character were foreshadowing the sexual revolution that would follow in the 1960s. The Pill would become available in Britain on the NHS in 1961. This was a significant revolution in itself. It meant that women, and couples, could now have sex without the constant fear of pregnancy — just like the women in a Bond story.

It was a revolution not just of the bedroom, but of the loosening of old social and class certainties, an upheaval of mores and attitudes. There was an irony to all of this: James Bond was the invention of a deeply conversative-minded author; Fleming had created this violent and unorthodox agent to be the fictional defender of the old guard and the established order. Now his invention was about to become an icon for an age that stood against that established order, that celebrated a classlessness and permissiveness in this 'let it all hang out' decade.

ALL I'M OUT FOR IS A GOOD TIME; THE REST IS PROPAGANDA

But those rumbling social changes were not loud enough yet to convince any financiers or studios of the potential of a Bond film. Saltzman soon ran into the same attitude articulated by Jack Warner, just before he walked out of a screening of *Look Back in Anger*. Americans, the primary source of funding for his proposed films, spoke American and they did not take too kindly to Limey speak.

Harry reached out to all his film contacts to come on board with Bond, but he was met with the same responses that had bedevilled all the previous attempts to bring Fleming's hero to the screen. The executives said the stories were just too violent, too sexual, and too English.

With his six months option close to its expiry date, Saltzman was still finding it difficult to raise capital. In May 1961, his friend, British screenwriter Wolf Mankowitz, suggested that Saltzman should have a meeting with another north American producer who was working out of London. Wolf knew that this producer was a fan of the Fleming books and, like Harry, believed in their screen potential. Saltzman wasn't about to hand over his option rights to another producer, but he needed to do something. He agreed to meet up with Cubby Broccoli to see if this might show a way forward.

Saltzman had not been the first producer to try and buy the film rights for Bond. As early as 1958, Ian Fleming's agent had been contacted by Broccoli; a New York Italian who, along with his business partner, Irving Allen, ran London-based Warwick Films. Their company had been churning out a string of solid, workmanlike British action films, usually with an imported American star taking the lead role. Broccoli had been a fan of the Bond stories since Fleming started producing them in the early 1950s. He was convinced the books had all the right ingredients of a successful movie franchise. Beautiful women, action, espionage, violence, sex, high stakes and exotic locations. However, his prickly partner Allen couldn't see any screen potential in these adolescent British spy stories.

Despite Allen's reservations, Cubby pushed ahead with setting up the meeting with the author, which was scheduled to take place at Les Ambassadeurs. It was an appropriately glamourous setting for a meeting to discuss the stylish, wager-loving Bond. However, Cubby's then wife Nedra fell seriously ill in New York and was taken into hospital. Broccoli jumped on a plane to be at her side and left the Fleming meeting to his partner. The duo, who had been making films in Britain for a few years now, had very different temperaments. Cubby was seen as the nice guy. The affable, lovable fellow who knew the names of everyone on the film set and would always ask after their wives and children. Allen was a very different kind of producer. He was autocratic and could be blunt — very blunt — if not downright rude.

Anthony Newley, the English actor, singer and songwriter, had appeared in a few Warwick Films, including *How to Murder a Rich Uncle*. He had his own take on the relationship between the pair. 'Cubby's job was to walk behind Irving, saying: "I'm terribly sorry, he didn't mean that".' Unfortunately, Cubby was not there to walk behind Irving the day he arrived at Les Ambassadeurs to sit down with Fleming and his agent. When Fleming's representative suggested an option for six books could be got for $50,000, Allen replied 'Come on, how can you talk figures like that? I'm sorry gentlemen but these books aren't even television material.' It was a short meeting.

Cubby would make a further failed attempt to get himself into the Bond act. Earlier in the decade Fleming had sold the film rights in perpetuity for *Casino Royale* to American producer and director Gregory Ratoff. Ratoff died before he could do anything with the option and Cubby tried to buy the rights to Fleming's first novel from his widow, but she turned him down. It seemed like all hopes Cubby entertained for translating Bond to the big screen had come to nothing.

Harry Saltzman made his reputation in British cinema by producing gritty 'kitchen sink' dramas including John Osborne's *Look Back in Anger* (1959).

4 Not even good enough for television

L ike his future partner, Harry Saltzman, Cubby Broccoli came from immigrant stock. His maternal grandmother, a widow from Calabria in southern Italy, arrived at Ellis Island with her three children in 1887. Her eldest daughter married another Italian immigrant, Giovani Broccoli, a construction worker twice her age. Their second son Albert Romano Broccoli was born in 1909. It was a breech birth and the child had trouble breathing. To treat his condition, they employed a traditional remedy from back home. Pushing the head of a black chicken into his mouth.

His nickname was given to him by his cousin Pat DiCicco. It originated from a popular comic strip character of the time, a little round fellow called Abie Kabbie, which got shortened to Cubby. Cubby would maintain that he was a descendent of the farmer who gave his name to the vegetable. The family worked on his uncle's farm while Cubby's father scraped the money together for his own small holding. They couldn't afford farmhands, so all the family joined in the back breaking field work, including young Cubby.

One day, May 20, 1927, to be exact, Cubby was working in the fields when he spotted in the sky a single engine monoplane, flying low because it was carrying too much fuel. 'I could see the name of the plane, *Spirit of St. Louis*,' remembered Cubby. 'I could see the pilot in the cockpit. I waved to him. He waved back. I remember thinking, If he ends up in the drink, I'll be the last human being to see Charles Lindbergh alive, but I know he's gonna make it, he's gonna fly the Atlantic all alone.'

Cubby maintained that the incident inspired him on to greater things. 'Believe in yourself, aim at the big horizon,' he told himself. After his father died, Cubby drifted through a number of jobs, including a stint working in a funeral parlour. Like his future screen star Sean Connery, he had put in his time polishing coffins.

His cousin Pat had decided that he was not farmer material and headed out West. For many of the poor émigrés who arrived in America, from Ireland, Italy, Poland and Russia, as well as their offspring, there seemed to be only two routes to realising the American dream: one was crime and the other was show business. Pat DiCicco would follow both paths. In Los Angeles, Pat would set himself up as an agent and sometime producer but, in reality, he was the right-hand man in Hollywood for New York mob boss Lucky Luciano.

Pat quickly became friendly with the leading figures in the film industry and allegedly provided them with women and drugs. He had a short-lived and volatile marriage to the actress Thelma Todd, which ended in violence and recrimination. After their divorce, Thelma would be found dead in her car at her home in Pacific Palisades, California. Her death will be officially labelled a suicide by carbon monoxide poisoning.

When he invited his cousin to visit, Cubby fell in love with all the Hollywood glamour, and he stayed. He found employment as a nightclub bouncer and door to door salesman while he tried to figure out an entry point into showbusiness. It helped that his cousin introduced him to the likes of Cary Grant and business magnate turned filmmaker Howard Hughes.

One of the strangest incidents in Cubby's pre-war years of struggle in Hollywood was an altercation involving Pat, Cubby, the actor Wallace Beery and a man called Ted Healy. Healy was a former Vaudeville performer and actor who was credited with creating the Three Stooges. He died in December 1937, after an evening drinking at the Trocadero nightclub on Sunset Strip. A spokesman for MGM, the studio that employed him, initially announced the cause of death was a heart attack. There was some bruising on his face and body which was initially put down to a fight in the car park with some 'college boys'. But other sources claimed the assailants were not college boys but Cubby, Pat and Beery. Broccoli admitted that he had been involved in a fist fight with Healy at the Trocadero, but later modified his story, admitting to pushing a drunken Healy, but not striking him. The Los Angeles County coroner would report that Healy died of acute alcoholism and the police closed their investigation. There was no indication in the report that physical assault played a part in his death.

With Pat's assistance, Cubby found work as third assistant on film sets, acting as a gofer for the director and escorting the actors from their trailers to the set. It is highly probable that without his connected cousin, Cubby Broccoli would never have settled into a career in film making. One of those early jobs was on the set of *The Outlaw*, a Western that would become one of the most controversial films of the forties. The original director Howard Hawks left the production after two weeks and its producer, the eccentric Howard Hughes took over the production. His obsession with filming the breasts of his leading actress, Jane Russell, would lead the film into controversial waters for violating the Hays Code, the self-censoring system among the

Hollywood studios, and delay its release for years. Cubby developed a friendship with Hughes which in no way harmed his ambitions to become a player in Hollywood. Around the same time, he married starlet Gloria Blondell, sister to the more famous actress Joan.

After spending the war years working for the entertainment division of the US Navy, Cubby returned to Hollywood but struggled to find a new niche for himself. His cousin stepped in again and found him work as production manager on a film called *Avalanche*, directed by Irving Allen and produced by Pat. It was a commercial and critical failure and, if that were not enough, around the same time Cubby's married failed. At his lowest point, he was selling Christmas trees by the side of the road. Later he got involved in a new business venture; an attempt to introduce the sport of motor racing to Europe. It brought Cubby to London for the first time. He was due to meet someone in the pub and stopped a man in the street to ask where was a pub called the Kings Arm? The man replied: 'around the Queen's Arse'. Cubby fell in love with the city. Nevertheless, the motor racing venture was a bust.

Back home in the States, he established himself as an agent with one of the major agencies, representing the likes of Robert Wagner, Ava Gardner and Lana Turner. He married again to a former model and actress Nedra Clark and, finally, he had a proper foothold in the film community. But Cubby's real ambition wasn't satisfied with being on the side lines. He wanted to be the guy producing the films. If he was going to make that leap into production, he needed a project. He found a book which he figured would make an excellent entree into the business. *The Red Beret* was an account of the British Parachute Regiment's exploits during the war. He approached a filmmaker he had worked with before, Irving Allen, about collaborating on turning this into a movie.

Since the disappointment of *Avalanche*, Allen had moved on and actually won an Oscar for his short, *Climbing The Matterhorn*. Irving was very much an old style and somewhat dictatorial filmmaker, a real hard-nosed showman. Together they created a new company. Warwick Films, named after the New York hotel where they struck the deal. Despite Allen's Oscar success, the pair were having trouble getting financial backing for their feature idea. They approached Richard Todd about playing the lead role in the film. The Irish-British actor had seen actual military service in the war, taking part in the D-Day landings. He found the book trite and unrealistic, and passed.

Like that other north American producer Harry Saltzman, the pair started looking at the incentives for filmmakers to set up shop in Britain. The Joseph McCarthy led witch-hunt targeting so called 'Reds' in Hollywood was in full flow. The pair figured that, along with the tax incentives, they might find more creative freedom and greater control over their films if they were operating at a distance from Los Angeles. The same year Fleming sat down to write the first Bond novel at his Jamaican retreat, Cubby was on a plane to London, to begin a new life and a new career.

The Eady Levy was a tax on box office receipts, designed to ensure that British films would be made, and they would be made using British actors and British crews. The British film technicians were professional and talented. The country had a world-renowned theatrical tradition and there was a host of trained, experienced actors looking for work. It did no harm that the crews and actors were also considerably cheaper than their American counterparts whose condition and salaries were now negotiated by powerful film unions. From the start, Broccoli and Allen established a formula which would be used on the majority of their 'British' film output. They would persuade a major Hollywood name to fly over and play the lead role in a film, surrounded by a solid cast of British actors in supporting roles and using British crews and technicians. That meant they could legitimately claim the film was, in the main, a British production and so access the all-important Levy funding. It also meant they were, potentially, producing films that were not so overtly British that they couldn't play to audiences in the drive-in cinemas of Ohio and Texas. Here were two producers who didn't need Jack Warner to tell them that US audiences wanted to hear actors on their movie houses speak American and not English.

In the 1950s, Columbia Pictures was developing a lucrative relationship with British-based film makers, backing, and distributing their product. This included Hammer Films which had cornered the market in Gothic horror and fantasy films. The studio would soon start a working relationship with Carl Foreman, one of a number of blacklisted filmmakers who escaped Hollywood for new careers in England. Foreman would help script the classic *Bridge Over The River Kwai*.

Columbia agreed to provide backing for Allen and Broccoli's films if they could put together the right package. The biggest box office draw at the time was Alan Ladd, and he was now their key target. Broccoli, the former agent, knew Ladd had just parted from Paramount over money disputes. Sue Carol was a powerful agent who had discovered Ladd and directed his career to the top of the box office. Along the way he became her fourth, and final, husband. Cubby focused on getting Sue to agree to Ladd signing a generous three picture contract with Warwick

Films, with the films being made outside the US. What they needed now was to set themselves up in England.

As a rather prosaic article in the British magazine, Kinematograph Weekly, put it a few years later the Allen and Broccoli story began 'in the year 1952 when the two American film men arrived on these shores with nothing but a piece of paper with Alan Ladd's signature written on it.' As part of the deal with Ladd and his wife, the producers agreed to employ his favourite writer. Richard Maibaum was an American screenwriter and producer who had worked closely with Ladd on several of his most successful films, including *The Great Gatsby* and *Captain Carey, USA*.

Maibaum would move with his family to London to work on scripting the Ladd projects. He would go on to become a regular at Warwick Films, and a key player in the Bond story. The story they wanted to tell was based on a real-life wartime raid carried out by the British Parachute Regiment on a German radar installation in northern France. The producers knew they had to tread carefully with their American lead. In the years after the war, there was growing cynicism about Americans taking credit for British war efforts, particularly in Hollywood films.

A few years earlier, one of Errol Flynn's most successful films, *Operation Burma*, had to be withdrawn from British cinemas because audiences were outraged at how the story side-lined British soldiers' involvement in this arena of the war. To get ahead of any criticism, Ladd's character was rewritten as an idealistic American who, before the US's entry into the conflict, pretends to be Canadian to enlist and join the fight against the Nazis. The producers made sure to employ members of the real Parachute Regiment as extras in their production. The director they chose, Terence Young, was a war veteran who had been an intelligence officer attached to the

Guards Armoured Division and had seen heavy fighting at Normandy and Arnhem.

The majority of the British war films at the time were made in black and white, but *The Red Beret* was going to be shot in Technicolor. Young and the film's cinematographer, Ted Moore, would be members of the crew who would go on to play crucial roles in bringing Bond to the screen. In one scene in *The Red Beret*, British actor Leo Genn, playing a unit commander, enters an office and tosses his beret onto a hat rack on the other side of the room. Young would remember the cool move and use it again for Bond as he enters Miss Moneypenny's office in *Dr No*. The film cost $700,000 and made $8 million worldwide. It was enough of a success to satisfy Columbia and ensure Warwick Films got to continue making movies.

Broccoli explained the guiding philosophy for their company: 'We're not making British pictures, but American pictures in Britain. We're trying to Americanise the actors' speech in order to make the Englishman understood down in Texas and Oklahoma. In other words, break down a natural resistance and get our pictures out of the art houses and into the regular theatres. And we're doing it. Furthermore, we'll soon be shooting all over the world, bringing to the public the beauty and scope of the outdoors in new mediums, real backgrounds, but always with an American star.' The duo moved into offices in South Audley Street in Mayfair, and they sat at a pair of vast desks, directly opposite each other.

Warwick's next film with Ladd was *Hell Below Zero*, based on a Hammond Innes novel. When the captain of an Antarctic whaling ship falls overboard in mysterious circumstances his daughter, aided by a sympathetic American, played by Ladd, decides to investigate. The film was shot partly in Pinewood. However, in line with Cubby's vow to bring 'the beauty and scope of the outdoors' to the public, this was a film that required some real ocean-based location shooting. They hired an icebreaker and rendezvoused with a real whaling fleet out in the Antarctic. Broccoli and Irving may have been partners, but Cubby was definitely the junior member of the team. And it was much more likely that he would be the producer who would be out on location, keeping an eye on the crew, the budget and the schedule. So, it was Cubby who accompanied the film unit for three months as they collected footage in Antarctic waters. He was totally unprepared for what it would take to shoot whaling footage in sub-zero temperature.

'I've learned one thing from this job,' stated Broccoli. 'It's a smart producer who selects a drawing-room background for any picture he plans to make.' It wasn't a lesson that was too deeply imbedded. In a few years, he would set off on an odyssey of producing a series of movies that would take him and his crew to every far-flung corner of the earth. Their third and final film with Ladd was a disappointing medieval saga which saw the American badly miscast at a sword maker in the court of King Arthur. It was again shot at Pinewood, and on location in Wales and Spain.

The British actor Donald Sinden had the next-door dressing room to Ladd at Pinewood. He particularly remembered that the American star's constant entourage included his stunt man, who bore an uncanny resemblance to him. Sinden said: 'The double did all the long shots, most of the medium shots and even appeared in two-shots when the hero had his back to the camera. The 'star' only did eleven days work in the entire film. He was extremely short in stature and unless he was alone, the camera could never show his feet because, if he was stationary, he was standing on a box. If walking, the other actors were in specially dug troughs or ditches and for anything between, all other actors were required to stand with their legs apart and their knees bent.'

The three films with Ladd were hardly classics but they helped establish the producers. By the middle of the decade, Warwick Films could justifiably claim to be the largest independent production house operating in Europe, and potentially its most successful. They now had the budgets and the ambitions to produce big adventure films with exotic locations. Among the Warwick output was *Fire Down Below*, this time starring a trio of Hollywood names, Rita Hayworth, Robert Mitchum and Jack Lemmon. It told the story of two rival riverboat captains who fall for the same woman. It was filmed in Trinidad and Tobago with Cubby, once again, the producer on location. He even made a rare, brief cameo on screen as a smuggler.

Hayworth had tried, unsuccessfully, to sue Columbia to extract herself from her contract. This was the first movie she made for the studio after she lost the court battle and she made her unhappiness known, creating a difficult shoot for her co-stars and producers. The budget was $2.5million, Warwick Films' biggest production so far, and it would fail to recoup its costs at the box office. Irving was content not to leave the Mayfair office if he could help it, which was probably just as well. Another Warwick production was a war time drama, *Cockleshell Heroes*, about a team of Royal Marines working behind enemy lines.

As per the Warwick policy, a Hollywood name had been brought in to ensure the film would have an American distribution and audience. Jose Ferrer, who had won an Oscar for *Cyrano De Bergerac*, was badly miscast as the leader of a unit. Allen had deigned to leave his desk and come down onto the location set, midway through the production. When the director, lead actor and the producer were watching rushes, Allen made some caustic comment about what they were seeing on the screen. Whatever it was, Ferrer took immediate offence and was so incensed he stormed out. The actor was eventually persuaded to return to the set and finish the film, but he never spoke to the producer again.

Of the producing partnership, Allen had a reputation for being cantankerous, abrasive, quick tempered and rude. Cubby could lose his temper, but it was a rare occurrence. Most of the time he was sweet natured, kind and attentive. It was a relationship that could almost have been a template for Cubby's next producer marriage. Maybe to prove they could do more than make war and action films, in 1957, they produced *How To Murder A Rich Uncle*, an adaptation of a French stage face. It starred the American character actor Charles Coburn as a rich Canadian, Uncle George, who visits his impoverished relations living on a dilapidated English country estate.

The cast included Anthony Newley and there was a small, comic bit part for a young up and coming actor. An unknown Michael Caine had been sent by his agent to the South Audley Street offices to discuss his suitability for the role. When he got there, he found he was up against another actor for the part, a one-time body builder and fellow out of work thespian. Cubby walked in and interviewed them both and, to Caine's great relief, he chose him over Sean Connery. The incentives offered by the British government to encourage film makers included productions made in parts of its colonial territories. Not surprisingly, this attracted Warwick's attention. Their action-adventure film, *Safari*, was filming on location in Kenya and set against the very real and present terrors of the Mau Mau uprising.

Victor Mature had been signed up for a two-picture deal with Warwick and was badly miscast as a big game hunter whose son, aunt and servants are all massacred by the Mau Mau. He then uses his big game hunting skills to track down the terrorists and exact revenge. Another American, Janet Leigh, played his love interest and Terence Young was again directing. Perhaps the most noteworthy thing about the film was when the second unit was actually attacked by the real-life Mau Mau.

Mature, who prided himself on being a devout coward, always had two guards with him. When the crew moved into the bush for shooting, he insisted on sharing a tent with Cubby. He figured if anyone was going to be safe from harm it would be the producer. When asked to wade into crocodile-infested waters to rescue Leigh, Mature insisted Cubby jump in first. Mature's misguided casting wasn't the only thing wrong with the picture. The whole film was misjudged, taking the real-life and ongoing horrors of the terrorists, and trivialising them as the backdrop for a B Movie.

The review in the London *Times* was damning: 'Surely it is neither priggish nor pompous to find something disagreeable in the idea of so horrifying an episode as the Mau Mau terrorism in Kenya serving as material for a film whose purpose is solely to entertain. A film that leaves an unpleasant taste in the mouth.' But then, Warwick Films was not in the business of making movies for snooty reviewers or the festival circuit. As Broccoli said: 'We try to make entertainment for the man who sits in the seat because he's the critic, he's the judge. The theatres are full of critics. They like this kind of picture because it's escapism and they identify themselves with what's on screen. We know this. They don't want to be identified with any political arrangements or any political figures.'

As the rota of Warwick Films' productions grew, Broccoli and Allen assembled a team of writers, technicians, directors and actors that they worked with time and again, building an almost familial sense among their regular talents. Along with directors like Young and writers like Maibaum, there were actors who had become Warwick regulars like Bernard Lee and technicians like set designer Ken Adam and cinematographer Ted Moore. When Broccoli did finally get his shot at Bond, he would have a solid bank of established film talent that he knew and trusted to lean back on.

The relationship between the two producers was becoming more strained, as it became cleared that each one wanted to focus on very different types of film. There were other dramatic changes in Broccoli's life. His wife Nadra had died from cancer, and he was left with two children to raise. His friend Cary Grant invited him to a New Year's Eve party stateside. While there he met a young actress and screenwriter Dana Wilson. They started on a whirlwind romance, and he married her in 1959, with Cary as his best man.

Warwick's next film, *The Trial of Oscar Wilde*, would turn out to be the swansong for the company. Broccoli may have insisted to the press that his film projects were aimed firmly at audience members in Oklahoma rather than the critics, but for their final film together he and Irving went for a cerebral 'quality' picture rather than another shoot 'um up action movie or war drama. It was also a controversial subject matter. A sympathetic drama that centred around the court case involving Oscar Wilde's homosexuality which destroyed his career and his life. The producers would be backing this film themselves. Maybe here was a Warwick Film production that even the critics might enjoy.

The Australian born actor Peter Finch was recruited to play the titular role. Finch had a personal obsession with the Irish playwright and would recite his poetry during breaks in filming. Robert Morley played the Marquis of Queensbury, who brought about Wilde's downfall. No sooner had they started pre-production than they learned a rival Wilde film was in the planning. The race was on to get their film ready and into the cinemas ahead of the competition. The shoot was a crammed six weeks. Then the producers set up four cutting rooms, with teams of editors working around the clock, just to get their feature finished first. In the end, both Wilde films opened within a week of each other in London. Neither performed well at the box office although Warwick did have the comfort that their film was a critical triumph and Finch would go on to earn a Bafta for his performance.

Bringing their story to America was another minefield, because of the film's sympathetic treatment of Wilde's homosexuality. The US distributors objected to one courtroom exchange in particular. Wilde is in the witness box and declares that he didn't kiss a male valet on the grounds that he was too ugly. The distributors wanted it cut. Cubby refused. Without that crucial scene the entire prosecution case — and the entire film — made no sense. In a rare display of religious unity, Protestant, Catholic and Jewish organisations in America all came out to attack the film. It was denied a general release and could only be screened at the art house cinemas in the States. It garnered good reviews but failed to attract an audience. It was an enormous blow for Cubby and a financially dismal end for Warwick Films.

The producers had been bickering more over the past few years and both wanted to focus on very different projects. Cubby, always the junior partner since the start of the union, was now eager to go it alone. The Wilde film won a prize at the Moscow Film Festival, but he had lost a lot of money on the project. Cubby declared: 'I decided I wasn't a philanthropist. You can win prizes, but you can't eat them.'

The achievements of Warwick Films were never fully recognised during its lifetime. With Hollywood backing, they produced a whole range of films that helped change the shape of British cinema and shake up the comfortable notions that had dominated it. The two producers were among the first north American producers to come over and set up shop in Britain. They led the charge over the Atlantic that would soon include filmmakers like Foreman, Stanley Kubrick and Sam Spiegel.

After the break-up, Cubby was left near broke, and he seriously considered moving back to the States with his now pregnant wife Dana. Instead, he stayed in London and, somewhat surprisingly, the producer duo continued to share their office in South Audley Street, planning their individual productions from the same space. Cubby floundered about what would be his next project. He toyed with bringing some of the Dickens' novels to television. He commissioned British playwright and novelist turned screenwriter Wolf Mankowitz to create a script based on the Arabian Nights stories.

However, by the time Wolf delivered the first draft, the producer had already lost interest in the project. 'Well, what exactly do you want to do?' asked an exasperated Mankowitz. What he really wanted, confessed Cubby, was to make a Bond film. But his former partner, Allen, had sunk that possibility years earlier after his disastrous meeting with Ian Fleming.

It just so happened that Wolf was also a friend and associate of the guy who now held the option on most of the Bond books. Harry Saltzman had the rights to most of the Bond catalogue, but he only had a month left to his six-month deal and he had not been able to interest any studio in the project. Perhaps Cubby could sit tight and then make his move to pick up the option when it lapsed, but it was a risky strategy. Saltzman might renew the option, or another producer might swoop in.

Wolf offered to set up a meeting between Cubby and Harry and found he liked the two men: 'They were both very easy to get on with. Saltzman was very intense, an extrovert, a Mike Todd-type of producer, while Cubby was very quiet with a solid, money background.' In exchange for his matchmaking duties, Wolf asked that, if the two men did strike some sort of deal together, he could come on board with scripting any Bond feature.

At the meeting, the two producers danced around each other. Harry tried to interest Cubby in a couple of other projects he was working on. There was a story about a guy getting rich in New York, and another one about a scarecrow coming to life. Cubby wasn't going to be distracted. He was focused on one story only. 'Don't bother,' said Harry. 'Nobody is interested in backing the Bond films.'

Cubby persisted, asking what he wanted for the rights. 'I told him I was only interested in Bond,' said Cubby. Saltzman had the option. but the clock was ticking down and he had no deal for distribution, no deal for production and no money. Despite his situation, Saltzman was not about the give up the rights. He suggested they join forces.

Broccoli, fresh from his divorce from Allen, was not exactly eager to slip back into a new partnership. There weren't too many north American film producers operating out of London for the past decades and it is highly likely that the two men were aware of each other's existence. It is equally likely that Broccoli was aware that Saltzman's temperament and blunt way of doing business were very similar to that of Irving Allen.

Cubby had a choice: he could simply let Saltzman's option just run out in a matter of weeks, and then approach Fleming for a new deal, but he might lose out again. Such was his desire to get his hands on the Bond property he reluctantly agreed to go into a partnership with this man he had only just met. Saltzman suggested a 51/49 partnership, favouring him. Cubby wasn't having any of it. It was 50/50 or no deal. They agreed and shook hands. Harry had exhausted all his film contacts with Bond, and nobody was interested. Now it was time for Cubby to take up the reigns.

Cubby Broccoli (pictured with Sean Connery) entered the world of movies thanks to his cousin, Pat DiCicco, who was the right-hand man in Hollywood for the New York Mafia boss, Lucky Luciano.

5 A rather silly British thriller

I t had taken years and involved him entering a marriage of convenience with another, belligerent producing partner, but Cubby Broccoli was finally in the Bond film making business. Now all he and Harry had to do was convince one of the major American studios to give them a large amount of money. Even Fleming allowed himself to think that this time, finally, his ambition to see Bond on the big screen was going to happen, possibly. He wrote to a friend: 'I'd seen (Saltzman's) *Saturday Night and Sunday Morning* and (Broccoli's) *The Trial of Oscar Wilde* and was very impressed. We discussed the project and I found them to be very intelligent chaps. I put my faith in them.'

From his years with Warwick Films, Cubby Broccoli had developed a solid working partnership with Columbia and, not unnaturally, they were his first port of call. Their response was frank and depressing. Bond, he was told, was a poor man's Mike Hammer and the character would simply not work for an American audience. An executive at the studio's New York office dismissed the James Bond oeuvre as 'a rather silly British thriller'.

Out of deference for their past working relationship with Broccoli, he was offered a deal which would have supplied him with a meagre budget a $400,000. The Bond stories involved exotic locations in faraway places, vast and complex lairs of the secret agent's foes and big explosive finales. That sort of budget was not going to cover the kind of movie they wanted to make.

After the disappointing response from Columbia, it seemed like Broccoli and Saltzman were facing the same impenetrable wall of received wisdom that had blighted Fleming and all those past would-be producers, directors and writers who had previously tried to bring Bond to the screen. It was always the same refrain from the money people: the Bond novels were simply too violent they said, or too sexual, or, above all, too damned English. The paperbacks of Bond might sell reasonably well in foreign markets, but a film version simply wouldn't work in the international field.

None of these executives could comprehend what Cubby and Harry had recognised. That here was a new type of British screen hero: sexy, violent, merciless, and amoral. Bond may work on Her Majesty's Secret Service, but he was very far from the old fashioned, clean-cut Rank Organisation matinee heroes that dominated post war British cinema.

Broccoli and Saltzman reckoned there was a global audience, ready for a cold-blooded, amoral hero, someone with a literal licence to kill. The next port of call for the producers was United Artists (UA). UA had been set up in 1919 by a trio of the earliest movie stars, Charlie Chaplin, Mary Pickford, and Douglas Fairbanks, along with director D W Griffiths. Their simple but revolutionary idea was for the creative talents to stop being the indentured servants of the all-powerful studios and take control of the means of production. It led one studio boss, Richard Rowland, to remark: 'The lunatics have taken over the asylum.'

The studio had gone through multiple crises since its inception. By the early 1950s it was in dire trouble and close to going out of business. At that point, entertainment lawyer Arthur Krim and his partners took control of the company and turned around its fortunes. Krim rebuilt its reputation with commercial and critical successes like *The African Queen, High Noon* and *Marty*. Under his management, UA also retained part of the studio's original mandate; to support artists and allow them to create without interference. Astutely, Krim and his team had figured out that the way to attract and work with the best talents in the film business was to provide them with a greater level of freedom than rival studios and trust that they knew what they were doing.

Among its other commercial successes was a series of Mike Hammer films. Hammer was the literary gumshoe created by Mickey Spillane, who had been such an influence on Fleming, and had been used over at Columbia to disparage his output. Broccoli called up the UA chairman and said he and his new partner wanted to fly over and pitch their exciting new project. He deliberately didn't give details, just in case Krim and his team had already made up their minds about the unfeasibility of adapting the Bond novels. Those executives hadn't heard Cubby's pitch on how it should be done yet. Krim said he and Saltzman needed to set up an interview with UA executive David Picker. On 20 June 1961, the pair arrived at the studio's New York HQ. Instead of the one or two executives they expected to be pitching to they found a boardroom full of top brass.

Picker had got wind from UA's London office that the producers had the option to the Bond novels and, unbeknownst to them, he was as excited about the character's screen potential as they were. Picker had been a fan of the novels since a relative recommended *Goldfinger*. He had even tried to interest Alfred Hitchcock in getting on board to helm a Bond movie.

The British director, who made a string of classic thrillers including *Rear Window* and *To Catch A Thief*, was at the top of his game. Indeed his 1959 film, *North by Northwest*, was an undoubted influence on the look and style of the Bond movies to come. In this story a suave, stylish protagonist survives assignation attempts, and falls for a girl who's secretly working for the enemy. He chases the bad guys across some visually stunning landmark sites until the finale at the top villain's secret lair. And all of this was done with a tongue in cheek humour. How could it not be an influence on future screen Bond?

However, when Picker got his office to enquire about the options rights on Bond a few months earlier they reported back that they were unavailable. And now, here were the producers who controlled the rights coming right to his door! When Saltzman announced they had the rights to the Bond books, Picker said: 'I didn't even try to hide my excitement. This was a deal I felt we had to make there and then.'

As his colleagues had not read the books, Picker took the lead in negotiations. A budget of $1 million was worked out for what they hoped would be the first production in a slate of Bond films. The producers' fees and profit share after UA had recovered its investment were all covered and sorted. 'Harry and Cubby understood the Bond books,' said Picker. 'They understood the kind of films we wanted to make, and they made them. The key to the film was spending enough money to maintain Fleming's tone in the sensuality, style, action and wit of the books.' They shook hands on the deal. UA were on board for a seven-picture deal. The meeting that launched the world's longest running and most successful movie franchise had taken all off 40 minutes. Director Terence Young, who would direct three Bond films, including the first one, said: 'I have to say I do admire David Picker at UA. David was the man who pushed this picture through.'

The ease and speed of the agreement left Saltzman nervous and confused. He simply could not believe they had come away with a solid contractual obligation, on the base of a handshake. He didn't understand, as Cubby did, that at the time a handshake with UA executives was as good as a signed contract. In the end, an embarrassed Broccoli had to go back into the UA office and get something on paper from them to appease the concerns of his anxious partner. Cubby then went to celebrate at the Morocco club in Manhattan with his wife Dana and to mark what was their second wedding anniversary.

The pair of producers formed two new companies to go along with their new partnership. Danjaq (an amalgam of their wives' first names, Dana Broccoli and Jacqueline Saltzman) would be based in Switzerland. Into this company they would invest all the copyright and future profits of the franchise. This would provide them with a highly lucrative tax advantage. It would be a 50/50 split between the producers, with their wives as non-voting minority shares. The production arm of the operation was to be called Eon Productions. Eon would actually make the films. They based the company out of Cubby's offices in South Audley Street. In years to come, they would be bemused to read that the production company name was chosen to stand for 'Everything Or Nothing', speaking to the great gamble the pair were undertaking. As far as they were concerned, Eon was just a name. It stood for nothing.

The producers now had the backing of a major Hollywood studio and, with Picker, a senior executive who was as passionate about the project as they were. All the same, the $1 million budget was modest, even by the standards of 1961. Saltzman was not making another one of his modest little kitchen sink dramas here. These were stories that demanded foreign locations, fabulous sets, big explosive scenes and armies of extras. The full contractual paperwork would not be completely formalised with UA until April 1962, after producers had finished shooting *Dr No*. And at the end of it, Fleming would earn a $100,000 per film and 2.5 per cent of the net profits.

There were other issues relating to the option that needed to be finalised urgently. Fleming, who was never in the business of making life easy for anyone, including himself, had spread the film rights across an array of family trusts. The producers needed to secure contracts that would ensure all parties were legally bound to their agreement and cover themselves against any problems down the line. In the end, Cubby and Harry found it made more sense to take over a London hotel for a day, assign an individual room for the beneficiaries of each trust and their lawyers and then go from room to room sorting out and signing their part of the agreement.

On 20 July 1961, the British film trade paper, *Kinematograph Weekly*, reported that 'Harry Saltzman's project with Cubby Broccoli to film the Ian Fleming spy thriller books is maturing nicely. They have clinched a deal with United Artists for 100 per cent financial backing and distribution of seven stories which will be filmed here and on foreign locations'.

Despite the modest budget, they knew they had found the perfect home for their Bond project. United Artists, the studio that had been created by actors and directors to give them greater creative freedom, still retained a reputation as being an artist-friendly business that did not try to interfere with the day-to-day production. Picker said: 'They had no obligation to report to us in any way, shape, or form if the picture was on budget and on schedule, because under the UA code of business they were free to make the movie as long as they use the script we approved, the cast we approved and the budget we approved.'

Eon had already begun the development of a script based on Fleming's most recent novel, *Thunderball*, which was published in 1961. Richard Maibaum, the American screenwriter who arrived at Warwick Films on the coattails of Alan Ladd and stayed on, was asked to work on the script. But by the time he delivered the first draft his producers had been forced to look to the other Bond novels for their screen debut.

Back in 1958, a mutual friend had introduced Fleming to the ambitious young Irish filmmaker Kevin McCrory with the idea of them collaborating on a Bond film. They decided that, instead of adapting any of the existing books, McCrory, working closely with Fleming and another writer Jack Whittingham, would develop an entirely new storyline for their screenplay, tentatively entitled *Longitude 78 West*. McCrory said it was a challenging creative process: 'He was upper class and Eton-educated. I was an uneducated Irishman, despite my experience. We clashed a lot.' When the trio were working on the script, at the tail end of the 1950s, it felt like the Cold War was finally beginning to thaw. Having Bond continue to battle against his regular enemy, SMERSH, the fictional Soviet counterintelligence agency, was starting to feel a little dated. Surely it made sense to find a new powerful, global enemy that Bond could take on. So, they created SPECTRE, an international conglomeration of crime organisations, headed by the mysterious Ernst Blofeld.

WHEN SEAN BECAME JAMES

In October 1959, the *Kinematograph Weekly* reported that McCrory had begun preproduction work on an underwater project with a working title of *James Bond of the Secret Service*. Inevitably, McCrory couldn't get the finance and the planned film project came to nothing. The writers all went their separate ways, and it looked like that was that. But Fleming was not a writer who liked to waste any material. He took the *Longitude 78 West* story and incorporated key elements of it into his next Bond novel, *Thunderball*. He did this without going to the effort of informing McCrory or Whittingham or including any acknowledgement of their involvement in coming up with the original story. Whittingham read a serialisation of *Thunderball* in a magazine and immediately recognised key elements of the screenplay he helped create. He alerted McCrory.

Thunderball was included in the option deal with Saltzman and Broccoli, but as soon as the book was published, McCrory started legal action against the author. It would be a long, drawn out and painful court battle for Fleming. One that he would lose and the stress of which may likely have contributed to his failing health. The legal proceedings also meant the producers needed to look at another novel to turn into their first screen adaptation. After briefly considering *Goldfinger*, they landed, in agreement with UA, on *Dr No*.

The novel had been roasted by the critics as one of the weakest Bond stories. However, using it as the first screen adaptation made sense financially. *Dr No* has only the one exotic location, Jamaica, and so would be less expensive to make. Picker said: 'The easiest one to do in terms of style and location was *Dr No*, so that's why I pushed for it.'

Cubby planned to use technicians and actors he had worked with during his years running Warwick Films.

Many of these would become regulars on the Bond franchise, reuniting every year or 18 months in some new foreign location, becoming a kind of 'Bond family'.

The producers and Fleming had another piece of good fortune that year. In March 1961, *LIFE* magazine published a list of President John F Kennedy's favourite books. In amongst the heavyweight political tomes and biographies was Fleming's *From Russia with Love*. Fleming had been selling well in the States, but this endorsement sent his sale rocketing and increased awareness of the Bond novels and character in the States. In the run up to the release of *Dr No*, Fleming approached Pan who published the paperback of the book and suggested they print an extra 500,000 copies. 'They laughed at me,' he said. But over the next 22 months the novel would shift a further million copies.

Five very different men from very different backgrounds collaborated (not always happily) to create the most successful film series in the history of cinema. From left to right: Cubby Broccoli, Sean Connery, Ian Fleming, Harry Saltzman and (not shown in this image) Terence Young.

6 I don't want my name on a piece of crap

After Alan Ladd's contract with Warwick Films ended, the man he had insisted be brought over to script his films, Richard Maibaum, stayed on in London. He became a regular scribe for Cubby's company, providing the script for *Zarak* and working on the screenplay for *Cockleshell Heroes*. Back when Cubby, and an unwilling Irving Allen, were considered the option on Bond, Cubby gave him some of the Fleming novels to read. Maibaum had advised against any deal. He enjoyed the books but thought the stories were too violent and too sexual to translate to the screen in the prurient and censorious 1950s. 'I liked them enormously,' said Maibaum. 'Cubby was very excited, too, but Irving Allen didn't share his enthusiasm.'

Irving won the day, effectively wrecking the meeting with Fleming. Maibaum said: 'It's my personal opinion now that that was a wise thing to do, because with the censorship of pictures that existed then, you couldn't even have the minimal sex and violence that we eventually put into the pictures. They just wouldn't have been the same.' However, with the onset of the 1960s, the climate around culture and censorship was noticeably changing. D H Lawrence's long banned novel, *Lady Chatterley's Lover*, was finally published in the UK, despite its graphic sexual content.

That publication was only allowed after a dramatic and ground-breaking obscenity trial, where the prosecutor's opening remarks to the jury posed the question: 'Is it a book that you would even wish your wife or your servants to read?' Well, not only were wives and servants now free to read Lawrence's graphic sex scenes but, in a few short years, they would also be free to laugh and be entertained by the sexual peccadillos and misdeeds of their betters, from the Duchess of Argyll to the Minister for War, John Profumo.

There was a new spirit of liberation, of pushing back at long-accepted boundaries of what was considered decent and acceptable. A small, poorly printed publication, called *Private Eye*, was launched in Soho in 1961 by a bunch of students. It poked fun at the establishment, and anyone else it thought worthy of satire, and ran the risk of libel with every fortnightly issue. One of its founders, a young Cambridge undergraduate named Peter Cook, had set up a new club, called The Establishment, which took political satire and turned it into entertainment. That would eventually lead to the launch of a BBC television series, *That Was The Week The Was*, which broadcast this new irreverence into the nation's living rooms.

Everywhere there was a sense of restless change, of casting of the old order, in theatre, in television, in music, in popular culture and in film as well. It had been a long decade of waiting for Ian Fleming, but maybe, just maybe, the public, and the censors appointed to oversee what the public could and could not watch, were now ready for screen Bond.

Maibaum worked on writing the first draft of the script from the *Thunderball* novel before seeing it abandoned after the McCrory legal action was launched. The Eon team needed to decide which novel they would adopt for their first Bond feature, and they needed to do it fast. Johanna Harwood was born in Ireland and ambitious to make her way in the movie industry as a screenwriter. She had studied in Paris and trained in the film industry in England before returning home to find work on Irish made films. The lack of opportunity in the small Irish film industry led her, inevitably, back to London. She did continuity work on several Warwick Films production, including *The Red Beret* and *Hell Below Zero*. She took work in the London office of a talent agency which at least gave her time to do her own writing. When a Canadian producer Harry Saltzman took over the offices, she stayed on as his secretary, eventually becoming his script reader and she persuaded him to let her write screenplays.

She produced two scripts for Windfall Films, including an adaptation of Colin MacInnes' cult London novel *City of Spades* which had been touted for production with Tony Richardson as director. That never happened but, as part of her writing side-line, Harwood produced short stories and one of them was a spoof of James Bond. *Some Are Born Great* was published in a childcare magazine, *Nursery World*, in 1959. It featured the Bond character playing a particularly intense card game, with the final reveal that the game was a round of snap, and 007 was actually a baby.

When Saltzman first obtained the option rights from Fleming, he asked Harwood to prepare treatments of the published novels. Johanna was not a fan of the *Dr No* novel but turned in the treatment document as requested. 'I thought it was one of the less good ones,' said Johanna. 'By this time, I think Ian Fleming was pushing it a bit.'

The producers were true to their promise to Wolf Mankowitz after he brought them together. Mankowitz and Maibaum were teamed up, given Harwood's treatment of *Dr No* and told to develop it into a full screenplay. Wolf, the son of a Russian émigré, was born in London's East End. After studying at Cambridge University, he began a successful writing career, first on stage and TV before graduating to film, scripting *Expresso Bongo* and *The Two Faces of Dr Jekyll*. He also adapted a George Bernard Shaw story into the script for *The Millionairess*, starring Sophia Loren and Peter Sellers.

The pair of writers were agreed on one thing. If this film was going to work, they needed to radically depart from the story of the *Dr No* novel, especially its central villain. Dr Julius No was a German Chinese psychopath with steel claws for hands. As far as the screenwriters were concerned, *Dr No* was nothing but an outmoded racial stereotype, a second-rate Fu Manchu. Their solution was to introduce a new foe for James Bond, a marmoset monkey. Their script played fast and loose with other parts of the novel's plot. The pair were quietly proud of their innovations when they presented it to the producers. Broccoli and Saltzman, however, were incensed at their radical departure from Fleming's story and Cubby did something which was rare for him: he lost his temper. 'You got to throw the whole damn thing out. No monkey do you hear!' he told them.

Wolf was convinced that sticking closely to the book's story and its cardboard villain would be a disaster and he bowed out of the project. He even asked for his name to be dropped from the screenwriting credits. 'I don't want my name on a piece of crap and that's a piece of crap,' he said. Maibaum produced a new draft that was closer to the book, and which contained no monkey villain. His other major bear bug with the novels was the lack of a sense of humour. He was able to inject at least some light moments into his scripted Bond, while adhering to the original story. It would be left to director Terence Young and his lead actor to enhance the humour, throwing in ad libs on the set. One thing that did survive from their drafts was the new scenes introducing the lead character to audiences. We first see the impeccably dressed Bond playing backgammon in an exclusive London casino and displaying his effortless way with women.

Maibaum would work on the scripts of a further thirteen Bond films, but his boss would never let him forget his initial brainwave. If there were ever future creative differences between him and the producer, Cubby would simply say: '*Dr No* is a monkey!' For his part, Mankowitz would soon regret his rash decision when he got to see the film at one of its pre-release screenings. He asked if his name could be put back on the credits, but by then the prints had already been made and it was too late.

Cubby had had years to daydream about what his Bond film would look like. He was very certain on what he wanted to see on screen. The movie would be a series of set pieces, almost like a collection of smaller movies within the larger film. For *Dr No*, there was the initial background setting up of the tale in Kingston. That was one story. Then on to London for the next small movie: the introduction of Bond, and the sending him off on his mission. Then Bond's arrival in Jamaica, the initial investigation and Bond battling the villain's henchman, and henchwomen. Then onto Crab Key island and the scenes in *Dr No*'s lair, the final battle between No and Bond and the destruction of all the villain had created.

In the South Audley Street office there were long and detailed discussions about every aspect of who this Bond character was. They wanted to know his psychology, his motivations, along with his brand of cigarettes, the Morland special blend with the three gold bands, just like the ones his creator smokes. What sort of lighter would Bond use? Did he wear cufflinks? Did he use suspenders? Did he have a tie pin? What about his cigarette case? His wallet? Did he wear a hat? What sort of watch hid he wear? In Fleming's novels, the agent wears a Rolex Oyster Perpetual. Cubby Broccoli wore a Big Crown Submariner 6538. He removed it from his wrist and handed it to Connery to wear when it was needed in shot.

Bond's civil service salary would be about $4,200 a year, not a bad wage for the era but modest considering his extravagant bachelor lifestyle. He had a stylish, comfortable flat in Wellington Square, just off The Kings Road in Chelsea, which was fashionable but not quite so expensive a place to live as it would become. Thankfully, while on his assignments, he had access to unlimited expenses. They scoured the novels for details, clues to his lifestyle. Perhaps surprisingly, Bond slept in pyjamas. He also abhorred shoelaces. And like Fleming, Bond was a gambler.

The scheduled commencement of filming was fast approaching. Broccoli was pulling together the crew and putting everything in place for the location shooting, while Saltzman was in charge of preparing the script and they still didn't have a working script. Saltzman handed the now revised script from Maibaum back to Johanna who was told to work with a new writer brought on board.

Aubrey Mather was the pen name of a career soldier, Jasper Davis. Davis had grown up in Australia and, seeking adventure, set off on an around the world trip. He landed in England penniless during the great depression and decided on a career in the military. He tried to enlist in the Royal Horse Artillery, but failed to gain a commission, and, in desperation, applied to join the Indian Army. He went on to carve out an impressive military career. In the 1950s, while still in uniform, Davis started writing short stories for magazines and newspapers, graduating to scripting dramas for radio and the emerging medium of television. He didn't publish his first novel until he was fully retired from the military at the end of the decade.

The Achilles Affair was an immediate best seller and his second book, *The Pass Beyond Kashmir*, an even greater success. His fans included Ernest Hemingway and Ian Fleming. It was Fleming who suggested Mather should have a hand in writing the script for *Dr No*. He was, figured Fleming, just the type of military minded, masculine author to beef up the action elements of the story.

Saltzman and Broccoli would take an option his Kashmir book, planning to make it with Connery and Honor Blackman starring. The project never progressed. Although offered a percentage of the profits for his work on the script, Mather opted, rather short-sightedly as it happened, for a flat fee. Mather also proved to be a bad fit. Saltzman was dismayed that the writer had the characters talking like Chicago hitmen. According to Johanna, none of his contributions made it into the final script.

It was near the end of 1961. Saltzman and Broccoli were just weeks away from the commencement of location shooting and the script was still not ready. In desperation, they booked director Terence Young and Johanna into a suite at a London hotel to work over the script. Young said: 'We took a room at the Dorchester Hotel, and we worked day and night.'

Harwood remembered Young's involvement rather differently. 'It was a joke really because what he had done was pretty well copied paragraphs out of the book,' said Harwood. 'There were great big swatches which said: "Bond thought hard about what he was going to do next!" Things you can't put in a picture at all.' She clashed with Young. When working together, he was largely dismissive despite her contribution to the finished film and in later years when discussing the making of the movie, diminished her involvement as a 'script doctor' or 'continuity girl'. Saltzman would have her contribute to the first three Bond movies as part of the writing team. She would be credited as one of the scripting team on the first two Bond films and uncredited for her work on the third.

Johanna's contribution to the first film is usually connected to the inclusion of a small but effective visual joke. In *Dr No*'s opulent apartment, Bond spots the Goya portrait of the Duke of Wellington. The original painting had been stolen from the National Gallery in London in August,1961. The daring theft had made news the world over and it had not yet been recovered. Over the decades since people have come to recognise Harwood's valuable contribution to the Bond history, which was certainly more than being a 'continuity girl'.

Although that final draft of the script was closer to the book, it did divert away from some of the more fantastic elements of Fleming's imagination. They kept in *Dr No*'s appearance and his background story, apart from one small detail: his steel claws were now metal hands. Also dropped was the giant man-eating squid that Bond was forced to battle against inside the villain's hideaway, and they lost a cage of tarantulas that novel Bond had to fight through. Johanna had been the one constant from the first initial treatment for *Dr No* to the last pre-filming script, dated 8 January 1962, and delivered eight days before principal photography was set to start in Kingston Jamaica.

It is perhaps ironic that one of the unsung protagonists of the chauvinist Bond franchise should be a young woman, who produced the first treatment of the story and was there working on the final draft of the script, but whose contribution has been side-lined.

7 Sir, am I going to be a success?

I t is 1957 and director Terence Young is struggling to complete location shooting on his latest film, an undemanding British-American drama called *Action of the Tiger*. The plot concerns an American contraband smuggler who is coerced into aiding a beautiful young French woman in a desperate bid to free her brother from an Albanian prison. American actor Van Johnson is woefully miscast in the lead role and there is zero chemistry between him and his leading lady, Martine Carol, who was one of the more provocative European sex symbols of the 50s, often tagged 'France's Marilyn Monroe'. According to a breathless report in the *Daily Mirror*, by the time she had signed on to *Action of The Tiger*, 'She has already made twenty-three films, overexposed in some of them, nude in one of them and taking baths in eight.' Action of the Tiger was not going to be a stretch of her acting abilities. She has two baths in this film.

A young unknown Scottish actor has a supporting role in the film. 'He was a rough diamond,' remembered Young. 'But already he had a sort of crude animal force, you know? Like a younger Burt Lancaster or Kirk Douglas. The interesting thing is that Martine Carol, who was a very famous French actress at the time, said, "This boy should be playing the lead instead of Van Johnson. This man has big star quality". Young regarded *Action of the Tiger* as 'a terrible film, very badly directed, very badly acted. It was not a good picture.'

When the day's shooting was completed, that bit part player came over to the director for some career advice. Young said: 'He asked, in a very strong Scottish accent, 'Sir, am I going to be a success?'

'I said, 'Not after this picture, you're not.' But I asked him, 'Can you swim?' Sean Connery looked rather blank and said, yes, he could swim, what's that got to do with it? I said, 'Well, you'd better keep swimming until I can get you a proper job and make up for what I did this time.'

Cubby Broccoli and Harry Saltzman had now secured studio backing and finance for their Bond film project. They and UA had finally agreed that the first film would be an adaptation of the novel *Dr No*. They had writers hard at work on a script, and they were leaning on them to ensure that it would fit closely with the storyline of the book.

While Saltzman was in charge overseeing that part of the process, Broccoli was signing up the crew for the production, including finding the best director for the job. Both producers knew the script was not quite there yet. What they really needed was a director who would be able to put his own shine and personality to it. They briefly considered hiring an American. Phil Karlson was making a name for himself making tough, realistic violent B Movies in the style of film noir, like *The Phenix* (sic), *City Story* and *The Brothers Rico* as well as the occasional Western. But he was too expensive for their modestly priced film and anyway, UA, which had to approve the director, were eager that a British talent take the helm. They wanted someone who intrinsically understood the world that shaped the writer Ian Fleming and in turn, helped shape and inform the character of Bond.

They approached Bryan Forbes. Forbes started out as an actor and got his writing break with Cubby at Warwick Films, co-scripting *Cockleshell Heroes*. He had just made his directing debut, *Whistle Down The Wind*, about a small group of children who find a criminal hiding in their family's barn and become convinced that he is Jesus Christ. The film was a critical and commercial success. Forbes had read the Bond books and he was definitely not in the fan club. He didn't want to offend Cubby by refusing the offer point blank, and instead excused himself by saying he had prior commitments. When he witnessed the success of the Bond franchise, he would regret his decision.

Guy Hamilton had learned the directing trade working with two of the greats of British cinema, Alexander Korda and Carol Reed. In the past decade he had shown himself a versatile helmsman, directing the successful wartime drama *The Colditz Story* alongside light comedies such as *A Touch of Larceny*, with James Mason and George Sanders. He even directed a musical, *Charley Moon*, with the English comedian Max Bygraves. Guy had not worked with Warwick Films, but he had a good friendship with Cubby who had tried to recruit him for several previous productions. However, the director had family commitments that meant he couldn't spend six weeks out of the country on location in Jamaica. He turned Cubby down, but he would go on to direct *Goldfinger* and several other Bond films.

The Oscar winning cinematographer turned director Guy Green also passed on the project. Val Guest, who directed *Expresso Bongo*, written by Wolf Mankowitz, was approached but not interested. Some of the directors were actually insulted that the producers might think they would deign to sign on for such a project. Finally, Cubby landed on someone who had been a Warwick Films stalwart: Terence Young had made four films for Warwick over the years of its existence and acted as an unofficial story editor for the company. Cubby's partner, Saltzman, was not sure about Young, and United Artists were equally dubious. Certainly, he was an efficient filmmaker, but he had a bit of a reputation for going over budget and having a leisurely attitude towards the necessarily tight schedules on film shoots.

Cubby stuck by his man. He figured Young would bring something unique to the project. And, in the end, after the job that been turned down by so many of his contemporaries Young was, effectively, the last man standing. It also didn't hurt that employing him was cheaper than many of his contemporaries.

Young was born in Shanghai from Irish heritage. He initially went to Cambridge to study for the priesthood, which obviously didn't work out. He excelled in sports and academics and in the pre-war years was regarded as one of the best screenwriters working in England. He also developed a taste for the sort of high society living that would define the rest of his life. Film editor Peter Hunt, who would build a close working relationship with Young on those early Bond films, said: 'Everything was the best. Terence always went to the best restaurants. He always drank the best wines. He always did everything better.'

When war broke out, Terence first tried to enlist in the navy. After they turned him down, he joined the Irish Guards. Young was a tank commander and participated in Operation Market Garden in Arnhem, an ambitious but unsuccessful attempt by the Allies to force an entry into Germany via the Netherlands. He was wounded and transferred to a Dutch hospital, where one of the volunteer nurses who took care of him was a young girl named Edda van Heemstra. She would become better known as the actress Audrey Hepburn. More than 20 years later Terence would direct her in one of her best roles, in the thriller, *Wait Until Dark.*

The director had much in common with Bond. He was public school and Cambridge-educated, as well as a military commander who'd had a 'good war'. Terence was also refined, elegant, witty, always impeccably dressed and a hit with the ladies. Broccoli's wife Dana said: 'Cubby knew that he would bring a lot of style to the film.'

Young had a steady but not spectacular directing career so far. After the war, he made his solo directorial debut with *Corridor of Mirrors*, a dark thriller that mixed gothic horror, fantasy and fairy tales. In the film, Eric Portman played a Bluebeard-like pirate character who seduces a young woman and transforms her into an ideal substitute for his lover from fifteenth century Italy. The film marked the screen debut of the actor Christopher Lee, who was Fleming's cousin, and would eventually go on to play one of the secret agent's most distinguished screen foes.

Corridor of Mirrors also starred Lois Maxwell, who worked with Young again on *Dr No* and on future Bond films as Miss Moneypenny. *Corridor of Mirrors* was named the Best Film of The Year Award in France and is now regarded a cult classic. In the years that followed, Young turned out a solid list of British B Movies, mainly focusing on war and action stories. He wrote and directed *They Were Not Divided*, a fictionalised account of three soldiers caught up in the campaigns that he had taken part in. The film interspersed documentary footage from the war and the cast included real soldiers with speaking parts alongside professional actors, including Desmond Llewelyn who played a tank gunner.

Young had been the natural choice for the Warwick Film producers when they arrived in London and were looking for a director for their first production, *The Red Beret*. Young had also directed *Safari* for Warwick Films, the adventure melodrama with Victor Mature playing a big game hunter in Kenya. The story took place against a backdrop of the Mau Mau uprising which was still going on when they arrived to shoot the film. The female lead, Janet Leigh, and some of the crew were attacked and robbed and a makeshift bomb went off outside Mature's hotel room. The plane carrying the films' wardrobe and props crashed and everything had to be replaced. Most of the crew caught dysentery and Young suffered badly from heat exhaustion but gamely continued to direct.

He also made *Zarak*, another challenging overseas location shoot with Mature this time playing an Afghan warrior who saves the life of a British officer. When they were filming on location in Morocco, the cast and crew were warned repeatedly to be sensitive to the customs and conservative sensibilities of the local Muslim population. It was advice that was ignored by the film's leading lady, Anita Ekberg. The Swedish actress went to the local kasbah by herself, dressed in shorts and a clinging top. She was soon surrounded by an angry mob, brandishing swords. Young rushed to the scene and had to use all his bearing and authority as a former military commander, as well as administering a few well-placed bribes, to get his leading lady to safety.

Young did turn his hand to subject matters and films that were less *Boy's Own* adventure and war. *Too Hot To Handle* starred American sex symbol Jayne Mansfield in a thriller that was billed as 'an exposé of sexy, sordid Soho, England's greatest shame'. Mansfield's see-through wardrobe and some racy musical numbers caused a bit of controversy, holding up the US release of the film. American audiences were not missing much. One review of *Too Hot To Handle*, in the Liverpool Echo, said 'The film will not enhance her (Mansfield's) reputation as an actress.'

Just ahead of the Bond gig, Young showed he could go highbrow. *Black Tights* was a French production telling four independent stories performed using the interpretative medium of ballet, interspersed with introductions by Maurice Chevalier. The film picked up the Biennale Special Golden Award at the Venice Film Festival and the European Grand Prix awarded by film critics in Europe.

Young had proved he was a capable director and a good man to have in your corner in a tight spot. He could even stand his own when facing down Ian Fleming's condescension. Young had known the writer through Fleming's wife Ann (formerly Ann Rothermere) and they shared a friendship with the playwright Noël Coward. Young remembered: 'We met just after I'd been signed to do the picture at some big press show put on by United Artists. Fleming said, 'So they've decided on you to fuck up my work'.

'I said: "Well let me put it this way Ian, I don't think anything you've written is immortal, as yet, Whereas the last picture I made won the Grand Prix at Venice".'

David Picker at UA at least recognised Young's unique qualities for the job: 'It was easy to say Terence was the living embodiment of James Bond, his style of dress, his style of life, he could have played James Bond himself.'

When Terence Young finally got out to Jamaica to commence filming on *Dr No*, his local guide was Chris Blackwell, a family friend of Fleming's. Even Blackwell recognised that the director brought a unique quality to the production. 'Terence Young was James Bond. He was the glamour.' But, right now, that location shoot — for a film whose script that was still under construction — seemed like a long way off. A brief news item in *Kinematograph*

Weekly in October 1961 said there would be no Bond movie shot until early 1962 because, 'No James Bond has yet materialised.'

Terence Young (pictured with Sean Connery and Claudine Auger during the filming of *Thunderball*) made a crucial contribution to Bond's success on screen. Lois Maxwell (Miss Moneypenny) recalled: 'Terence took Sean under his wing. He took him to dinner, to his tailor, showed him how to walk, how to talk, even how to eat.'

8 New York feel we could do better

Cary Grant was both a fan of the Bond books and a close friend of Cubby Broccoli. He had even been best man at his wedding to Dana. Nevertheless, Cary was also just a few years away from turning sixty, would be unlikely to commit to more than one film, and his usual fee would have consumed most of the budget for *Dr No*. Dana Broccoli said: 'Cubby knew if he asked Cary Grant, it would be a one picture deal and then he'd have to start all over again.'

In 2022, when Daniel Craig finally handed back his licence to kill, newspapers and websites knew they could fill a slow news day with speculation on who would be the new Bond. The ever-changing list would likely include pretty much every British, Irish, Australian and occasionally American lead actor who was in the right age bracket for the job. And because it's 2022, the list now runs through several leading actresses as well. That guessing game ritual is as old as the Bond franchise itself. In 1961 James Mason reportedly almost snagged the role and indeed, at one point, thought he had it. This was despite asking for more money than what was on offer from the producers. However, it was his insistence that he would only sign up to two films which cost him the part.

The Irish American actor Patrick McGoohan was already established as a serious actor on stage, screen and television. He was approached and considered a viable option by Saltzman and Broccoli. He'd previously worked with Cubby and director Terence Young on the Warwick film, *Zarak*. McGoohan was the star of the recently broadcast television series *Danger Man*. He played a British secret agent jet-setting around the world having adventures, who would introduce himself as 'Drake… John Drake'.

Ian Fleming had been briefly involved in the development of the *Danger Man* series before bowing out. It is unlikely the author would have approved of the direction it had taken, once McGoohan got involved. The actor was a devout Roman Catholic who made it a condition of his accepting the TV role that there would be no guns. His secret agent beats his foes using his brains not violence. Additionally, there would be no kissing, and no romance. It would be difficult to imagine bringing James Bond to the screen without the sex and the violence. It was hardly surprising that the role was not to McGoohan's tastes.

David Niven was considered, briefly. He was a favoured choice of Fleming. Niven certainly had some of the Bond qualities but lacked the physicality of the role. He would get the opportunity to play a Bond, of sorts, in the muddled rival production of *Casino Royale* a few years later.

Rex Harrison was considered and passed over. So was director Terence Young's favoured choice, Richard Johnson, who was making a name for himself as a Shakespearian actor. Johnson had to turn the role down as he was under contract to studio rival, MGM. He would say later: 'Eventually they offered it to Sean Connery, who was completely wrong for the part. But in getting the wrong man they got the right man, because it turned the thing on its head, and he made it funny. And that's what propelled it to success.'

Johnson would play an updated version of a more traditional British fictional hero, Bulldog Drummond, in *Deadlier Than The Male*. This would be just one of many Sixties 'lone agent' thrillers that would go into production on the tail of the Bond phenomena. Saltzman briefly considered a young actor who had been starring in a series of Hammer Films, a nephew of the director Carol Reed, called Oliver Reed.

The producers also approached the ruggedly handsome Australian actor Rod Taylor but he declined the offer to do a screen test. 'I thought it was beneath me,' said Taylor. 'I didn't think Bond would be successful in the movies. It was one of the greatest mistakes of my career. Every time a new Bond picture became a smash hit, I tore my hair out. Cubby and I have laughed about it ever since.'

Broccoli and Saltzman briefly considered casting an American. That would, at least, follow the tried and trusted formula of the Warwick Films of the 1950s, drafting in an American star for the lead role in an otherwise ostensibly British film. They looked at Steve Reeves, an American bodybuilder turned actor who'd become a screen favourite via a series of Italian made 'sword and sandals' epics in the 1950s. He wanted too much money and beside there was the shambles of the earlier television movie of *Casino Royale*, and the American 'Jimmie Bond' to bear in mind.

Fleming was eager for them to look at Roger Moore, who already had successes on US and British television. But Moore was about to take on the role of Simon Templar, a kind of freelance, secret agent nicknamed *The Saint*, adapted for television from a series of books from the twenties. Templar, suave, unruffled, a hit with the ladies and willing to work outside of the law for what was right, had more than a passing resemblance to Bond. The first series of *The Saint* would be broadcast within a few weeks of the premiere of *Dr No*. A decade later Moore would take up the 007 role.

Michael Craig, a promising young British actor was considered. He said that, at the time, Saltzman and Broccoli were close to joke figures in the British film industry. No one could quite figure out how they got the Bond film rights. 'I never actually auditioned for James Bond, but I was told that Rank, who I had a contract with at the time, were asked to loan me out,' said Craig. 'My agents had said to not even think about it. The production company's no good, the money's no good, the film will be no good. Agents, eh? I think Sean did the first one for peanuts. Back then, Cubby Broccoli and Harry Saltzman were very much B Movie producers, so they didn't have a good reputation. I'd never have been the 007 that Sean was and maybe there wouldn't have been more than that first one.'

It would seem easier to list those actors who were not, at one time or another, publicly linked to the role of Bond. Back in 1958, when Cubby had first been thinking about producing a screen Bond, and before his partner Irving Allen botched the meeting with Fleming, he had approached Peter Lawford, the one English member of Frank Sinatra's Rat Pack, but Lawford declined anyway.

The *Daily Express*, which had been serialising Fleming's stories in strip cartoon form, got in on the act by launching a nationwide competition to find the screen Bond. It had whittled down more than 1,000 entries to six, who were screen tested by Eon at Twickenham studios. Of the six finalists, one man emerged as a clear winner. Peter Anthony was a male model, often seen in cigarette adverts at the time. While he may have had the looks, Peter didn't have the acting ability. He was offered a small role in the Bond film when it was made. A part that never materialised.

In an interview with the *Sydney Morning Herald*, decades later, Broccoli would claim that they had, at one time, considered the infamous aristocrat Lord Lucan for the role. It sounds fanciful but both Broccoli and Lucan were avid gamblers. The pair were regulars at the same exclusive clubs, restaurants, and casinos of London, and shared many of the same social circle. Lucan was well known for his expensive lifestyle and dashing good looks. He even drove an Aston Martin.

'He had it all,' said Broccoli. 'The looks, the breeding, the pride. I seriously wanted to test him for Bond, but all he'd say was 'good heavens'. Lucan disappeared in 1974 after the murder of his children's nanny in his estranged wife's home in Lower Belgrave Street, just around the corner from Fleming's old bachelor pad in Ebury Street. Lucan remains the prime suspect in the brutal murder.

Saltzman and Broccoli knew that finding the right actor was crucial to the success of the film and the possibility of creating a movie franchise, but they were running out of options. And while they may have publicly been considering some of the most established and respected British actors of the era, what Saltzman and Broccoli really wanted was someone who could project a new kind of British hero. They needed a leading man who was sexy rather than paternal, arrogant instead of self-effacing, dangerous rather than protective, amoral as opposed to upstanding. So, basically, all the things your standard British screen idol of the 1950s was not. Also, they didn't have much money to spend on a big name. For all the talk about established marquee names like Grant, it is unlikely that they would be serious contenders for the role, any more than whoever won the *Daily Express* contest.

Saltzman and Broccoli were showmen after all, and like Saltzman's black soap trick from his young, huckster days, they knew they had to get the crowd interested in their latest project any which way. This constant speculation in the press over who would play Bond was useful in raising the profile of their modest little spy film.

For all of David Picker's enthusiasm, United Artists had set a tight budget for the production, and this was a story with an international location shoot, elaborate sets that would need to be built from scratch and explosive action scenes. All of that cost money and they had a budget of $140,000 to pay for the entire cast. Many of the star names they had been throwing around would easily have eaten up that casting budget. A relative unknown would allow them greater scope to create a new type of screen hero from the ground up. It would be easier to tie a less established actor into a contractual commitment to star in subsequent Bond movies if the first one took off. And he would also be considerably cheaper.

Harry and Cubby felt that many people, including all the studio executives who had passed on Bond, had missed the point of this special agent. All these movie professionals saw him as a hero of the old school. A suave, well-bred English gentlemen of charm, dressed in a tuxedo and always with a beautiful girl on his arm. Saltzman and Broccoli had operated out of London for the past decade but had an objectivity from being outsiders to the country and the class system that had formed Fleming and Bond. They saw Bond very differently, their Bond was more masculine, he was just as comfortable scrapping in a back alley as he was sipping cocktails in a casino. He was tougher, in his actions and in his thinking, and he was capable of cruelty and sadism. This was the 'blunt instrument', as described by his author, and that was what they were looking for:

a leading man who could convey all of that. 'If the films were successful,' said Broccoli, 'they would make whoever played Bond famous.'

In the first novel *Casino Royale*, Vesper Lynd, Bond's fellow agent, lover and eventual betrayer, tries to describe him. 'He is very good looking. He reminds me rather of Hoagy Carmichael, there is something cold and ruthless in his...' Vesper never gets to finish her sentence. An explosion smashes the window close to where she sits. Hoagy Carmichael was a languid, American musician, composer and actor who starred in a series of films of the 1940s, usually playing a version of himself. Carmichael had himself described his on-screen persona as a 'hound-dog-faced old musical philosopher noodling on the honky-tonk piano'.

There is often, among the cinema going public, a general confusion about what exactly it is that a producer does on a film. Cubby, in a later interview, would try to encapsulate the core of his role as producer, specifically as a producer of the first Bond movie. 'The prime contribution, and the producer's function, is to convince a distributor that the picture should be made of James Bond,' said Broccoli, 'because it had been over-looked for many years. And then that the picture should be made without any known actors in it was another obstacle.'

One night Harry Saltzman and his wife were at dinner party, held in the Polish Club in London. Among the other guests were the Polish born film producer Benjamin Fisz, and his English film editor Peter Hunt. The pair were just completing work on a low-budget flick, set during the war, called *On The Fiddle*. In the comedy, Alfred Lynch, a Royal Court Theatre regular, played a small-time crook who signs up for the RAF to avoid prison. He teams up with an affable sidekick, Pedlar Pascoe, played by Sean Connery, to carry out some further scams, but they accidentally end up war heroes. Fisz had initially not wanted to use Connery. The Scot had a supporting role in one of his previous films, Hell Drivers, and he didn't think much of his acting skills. However, that had been a few years ago, and once he saw the more experienced Connery at work on the set of Fiddle, he was impressed.

Saltzman was complaining about the difficulties of finding the right actor to play the central role in this film based on Ian Fleming's novels. Peter Hunt said: 'Ben suggested Sean Connery would make a very good James Bond.' Hunt ended up sending across a couple of reels from the Fiddle film for Saltzman to look at. 'Whether that influenced them or not, I don't know,' said Hunt.

Saltzman reputedly asked the film's director Cyril Frankel if he thought Connery could play Bond. His response: 'Standing on his head and reading a newspaper.' Around the same time Cubby was in LA watching a screening of a Disney B Movie with the unlikely title of *Darby O'Gill and the Little People*. Back in his agent days, Cubby had represented Lana Turner and they had remained friends. He'd visited her on the set of a film she made in London a few years earlier. And he remembered being introduced to the tall, handsome Scottish actor who played opposite her.

Broccoli had almost cast Connery in a tiny role in one of his Warwick Films a few years earlier, *How To Murder A Rich Uncle*. Connery obviously had not registered too well with him at the time, as he lost out on the part to Michael Caine. Darby O'Gill was a curious and whimsical tale about a wily, old Irishman who tricks a leprechaun out of his pot o' gold. Although set in Ireland, it was made entirely on the backlots of Hollywood. A second-tier storyline involved a romance between the old fellow's colleen of a daughter and a handsome beau with heavy set eyebrows and a decidedly strained Irish accent.

Broccoli was impressed by the Sean Connery he was seeing up on the screen, but he wasn't convinced he had what it took to play Bond. He called his wife Dana and said: 'I've just seen this actor and I think he's terrific, but I don't know if he has any sex appeal.' He arranged a second showing of the film with Dana by his side. After she'd watched it, she turned to him and said: 'Cubby, he's fantastic.'

Saltzman watched the scenes from *On The Fiddle* sent over by Peter Hunt, but still wasn't convinced they had their man. What they needed to do was meet the actor in the flesh. Sean remembered: 'Broccoli called and said he had this Fleming film and thought I might fit the part. He asked me over and we discussed it a bit further.' Connery read a couple of the novels and, although not a fan, he thought he had a good handle on what made Bond tick and how this character should be played. He was intelligent enough to recognise the role could be career changing, and life changing, and arrogant enough to believe that the part should be his. He showed the books to Diane Cilento, his actress girlfriend who would soon become his wife. Diane was blunt in her opinion: 'I found the dialogue stilted. The character of Bond effortlessly awful unless he was given a sublime sense of humour. The violence, and 'license to kill' stuff, could only be brought off if it was accomplished with a lot of ritualistic absurdity and fun.'

If there was humour in the early novels, it is not given to the lead character. Post Connery's appearance in *Dr No*, Fleming would inflect the Bond of his novels with more of a sense of fun. By his final novel, *The Man with the Golden Gun*, Bond would be much closer to the Connery version of the character. Sean was in agreement with his girlfriend's opinion. And he had his own unique ideas about how to approach the scheduled meeting with the two producers from across the Atlantic who were making the movie.

As part of his education, Sean had studied the Method Acting technique developed by Russian theatre director, Konstantin Stanislavski, and much in vogue with American screen actors. Sean was going to go full Method, immersing himself in his character's inner motivation and emotions, for this meeting with the producers.

He turned up at the South Audley Street office, dressed in baggy, unpressed trousers, brown shirt, lumber jacket, suede shoes and no tie. He put on a show of insolent, macho arrogance. All appropriate Alpha Male traits to bring to the secret agent role. At one point Connery became so adamant and so passionate about how Bond should be played he banged his fist on the table. This was not the way actors usually operate when they meet a pair of filmmakers who have it in their power to change the course of their lives.

Saltzman remembers: 'When he wanted to make a point, he'd bang his fist on the desk, or his thigh, and we knew this guy had something.' This display of arrogance worked. The producers were intrigued, but Connery hadn't finished with the Alpha Male posturing. 'I said I would be interested provided they put some more humour into the story,' said Connery. 'I felt this was essential. Broccoli agreed, then said 'When can you test' I asked, 'what for?' He said, 'a film test'. I said, "sorry but I'm not making tests. I'm well past that. Take it or leave it but no test". He watched as Cubby's face turned a shade of purple, but the producer kept calm and composed himself. 'He said he'd think it over and let me know,' said the actor. It could so easily have been a disastrous strategy for Connery. As he would confess later: 'I put on a bit of an act. And it paid off.'

After the meeting ended, Dana called her husband and

Harry over to the window and they watched Sean stride across the road to where he had parked his girlfriend's borrowed Fiat. 'He walks', said Dana, 'like a panther'. 'There's only one other actor who moves as well as he does,' said Broccoli, 'and that's Albert Finney. They move like cats. For a big man to be light on his feet is most unusual.'

Saltzman said: 'We'd never seen a surer guy. Nor a more arrogant sonofabitch. We spoke to him and saw that he had the masculinity the part needed. When he left, we watched him from the window as he walked down the street and we all said, "he's got it".'

They were all agreed then. They had found their Bond. Now there was just the small business of convincing everybody else. 'For a large man Connery moves extremely well,' said Saltzman. 'He had acting ability, he had experience, he was the right age. I might tell you we had a lot of opposition when we picked him from everybody.'

Connery himself already had his concerns about accepting the role. Yes, potentially it was an amazing opportunity. But then he had tied himself into a contract with 20th Century Fox because it felt like an amazing opportunity, and that ended in dismal failure. Sean was establishing himself, finally, as a serious actor. One who had acquitted himself well in some of the great plays of the theatre, working alongside leading lights of the stage, like Claire Bloom. Would playing this Bond character — 'a thug in a morning suit' as one critic called him — be a regressive step? What if it were a success and led to him being typecast? It was Diane who finally convinced Connery that Bond was too good an opportunity to turn down. She would later say: 'If it wasn't for me, Sean might never have become Bond.'

The producers first had to get the author on board with their choice. They decided on a strategy of sugaring the pill before fully introducing Connery to Bond's creator. It was a strategy that seemed to work, at least in the short term. At the time Fleming wrote to a friend about the search for a screen Bond: 'Saltzman thinks he has an absolute corker. A 30-year-old Shakespearian actor, ex-navy-boxing champion and even, he says, intelligent.' While none of that was not exactly untrue, it did not fully encapsulate the complete origin story of Sean Connery.

A meeting between the actor and the author was arranged in Fleming's office in Pall Mall. It was not a happy first date for Fleming. He had always envisioned Bond as not unlike himself: English public school, university-educated, high born, posh, and definitely not speaking with a Scottish burr. Fleming privately said: 'I thought I would be meeting Commander Bond, not an overgrown stuntman.'

As far as Connery was concerned the meeting went well. He discussed the role with the author and believed they saw the character in a similar light. 'There was certainly no dissention between us on how to see Bond,' said Sean. 'I saw him as a complete sensualist. His senses highly tuned, awake to everything, quite amoral. I particularly liked him because he thrives on conflict.'

The reaction from United Artists was not much better than Fleming's. A telegram from the United Artist executives to the producers, dated 23 August 1961, simply read: 'New York did not care for Connery feel we could do better'. Nevertheless, the producers were not going to be swayed. They knew in their heart of hearts they could not do better than Connery. And he was going to be their Bond.

Time and time again people had identified a quality in Connery's persona and his acting that wasn't quite British. He had an earthy, ballsy quality that set him apart from the classic British leading men, who were more likely to be well-mannered, refined, slightly effete, stage bound and gentlemanly. Connery was much more like an American movie star.

Sean was kept in the dark about how unhappy the UA executives were with the producers choosing him. He also wasn't told about the other actors who were still being auditioned for the role that he thought was definitely his. Despite his obstinacy, they tricked him into doing a screen test, telling him they needed to see him on camera against actresses they were looking at for the main female roles.

His screen test did nothing to convince the New York office of the wisdom of their choice. Cubby and Harry held firm. They said they would either go ahead with Connery or not do the picture at all. The producers did have an ally of sorts in Bud Ornstein who was based in UA's London office. His verdict on Connery: 'He is the best we have come up with to date.' It was hardly the most ringing endorsement.

A modest little news items in the *Daily Cinema* newspaper on 3 November 1961 announced the casting of Sean Connery in the role of James Bond in the upcoming production of *Dr No*. The shooting was scheduled to start January 1962 and they had just got in under the wire with their leading man. David Picker said: 'I think I heard the expression at the time, He (Connery) was the richest man in the poor house. The best choice that no one was jumping up and down about, but he was fine.'

Connery was to be paid a modest £6,000 for the role, plus £25 a day expenses, and, if the film was a success, contracted to make further Bond movies. Connery himself would say years later: 'It was a bit of a joke around town that I was chosen for Bond. The character is not really me at all. I talked a lot to the author of the Bond novels, Ian Fleming, and the director, Terence Young, about the physical aspect and also about my accent. I always had a terrible fight to get work in Britain on account of my Edinburgh accent.'

'I wanted a ballsy guy,' said Cubby. 'Put a bit of veneer over that tough Scottish hide and you've got Fleming's Bond, instead of the mincing poofs we had applying for the job.'

In 1964, Rex Harrison, who had been briefly considered for the Bond role, would win an Oscar for his performance as Professor Henry Higgins in *My Fair Lady*. In this musical adaptation of George Bernard Shaw's play *Pygmalion*, Professor Higgins accepts a bet to transform a cockney street flower seller into a refined lady who speaks 'proper English' and can pass herself off as a member of the high society of Edwardian London.

The Bond producers and their director for the film production of *Dr No* now had a similar challenge with their ex-bouncer and coffin polisher from Edinburgh; to, in Cubby's words, 'put a bit of veneer over that tough Scottish hide'. Their attempt at their *Pygmalion* transformation was about to commence.

Ian Fleming was initially opposed to the casting of Sean Connery as James Bond. 'He's nothing but an overgrown stuntman,' he complained.

9 No one would remember Columbus

S ean Connery is on the set of his latest film at Pinewood. It's his most substantial role yet. He's the male lead, playing opposite one of the most beautiful and acclaimed actresses in Hollywood, even if his character does die half-way through the film. The press legend has it that Lana Turner was the original Hollywood dream; discovered sitting by the soda fountain at Schwab's Pharmacy in Hollywood. The truth is only slightly less implausible. She was spotted buying a Coke in a local mall. In her first film, Lana had a small role playing a teenage murder victim. Because of the tight top she was given to wear — which accentuated her breasts — she got tagged the 'sweater girl'. It was a nickname she detested but, like the top, it clung to her.

By the mid-forties, she was one of the world's highest paid actresses. Her career has waned since then, but in 1957 she still retains all that star quality. In their film together, *Another Time, Another Place*, Sean plays a married BBC journalist who becomes the young lover of a visiting American reporter, played by Lana. Up until now, most of Sean's screen roles had been bit parts in small British films that relied on his physique and masculine good looks rather than any acting ability. It frustrated him that he was usually cast as a crook, or a heavy, or a truck driver.

136

He had only recently signed a seven-year contract with 20th Century Fox, a major Hollywood studio. This is the first role they found for him. To prepare for the part, he's spent hours listening to recordings of news reports filed by real broadcast journalists, from the BBC's Richard Dimbleby to the American wartime correspondent Ed Murrow. He won't get much chance to show off the research in the role, but that doesn't matter. What's important to him is that he did the work and threw himself into the part.

The presence of a bona fide Hollywood star at work in England is attracting a lot of press attention. Sean is irritated by reporters who keep asking him what it's like to play the lover of an older woman. It's ungallant and it's also just bloody rude. Lana was born in 1921, which makes her nine years older than Sean, not a massive age difference, but practically the Grand Canyon in movieland terms. He bats away the question. This is the beginning of a tense and problematic relationship with the media that would annoy the hell out of him for the rest of his life. The two are getting on well. 'I adored her,' said Sean.

One of the visitors to the set is Lana's former Hollywood agent who has now crossed over to being a film producer in his own right and bases himself in London. Cubby Broccoli remembered Lana introducing him to her co-star: 'He was a handsome, personable guy, projecting a kind of animal virility. He was tall, with a strong physical presence and there was just the right hint of threat behind that hard smile and faint Scottish burr.'

The public relations machine at 20th Century Fox has been dropping hints to tame reporters that the on-screen chemistry between the pair is, possibly, continuing off screen. It's an oft used studio trick to drum up some interest ahead of a film's release. Unfortunately, Lana's latest boyfriend, Johnny Stompanato, isn't familiar with the nature of showbusiness PR. He is a connected gangster who has started thinking of himself as a would-be film producer. He had been a bodyguard to the mob boss Mickey Cohen, and he's also an alcoholic and a jealous and violent thug who regularly beats up his girlfriend.

After hearing the rumour about his girl and this handsome young actor, he flies to London, arrives on the set at Pinewood, drunk, pulls out a gun and points it at Connery's chest. If the scene had been caught on camera, it might have served well as Sean's screen test for the Bond role. Connery removes the pistol from him, punches the mobster in the jaw and sends him sprawling onto the floor. Stompanato, humiliated, will take it out on Turner later, beating her up at the London house where she's staying. Eventually he is deported back to the States.

Even aside from the Stompanato incident, it has been an unhappy shoot. Connery keeps fluffing his lines and missing cues. Lana has to mediate between him and the increasingly irate director. Turner said: 'Because I was co-producer, I had to work to smooth things out to ensure that the schedule went ahead as planned.' When the film was finally released it was another disappointment for Connery. It was passed over by critics and the public. The *Sunday Mirror*'s assessment of the film was typical. It was, said the reviewer, 'fine for sobs.'

The melodrama that everyone was really fascinated by was not on the screen, but the one involving Lana Turner's private life. A few months after filming was completed and Lana was back in her Hollywood home, her daughter Cheryl stabbed Stompanato to death with a butcher's knife. She had heard him threaten to carve up her mother. Mickey Cohen, the mob boss and former associate of Stompanato, would pay for the hood's funeral and took out a media vendetta against Lana Turner, whom he blamed for the death.

NO ONE WOULD REMEMBER COLUMBUS

The was nothing in Sean Connery's birth or background suggesting that here was a future international movie star. He was born in Fountainbridge, an industrial area of Edinburgh where the main employers were breweries and a giant factory complex making wellington boots and wheels. 'The place smelled of rubber and hops,' remembered Connery.

He was born at 6.30pm on 25 August,1930 and christened Thomas, after his grandfather. As a baby he slept in the bottom drawer of a dresser in his parent's bedroom. Two of his paternal great grandparents had arrived in Scotland from Ireland. One of them had been an Irish Traveller. His father, Joseph, was a sometime labourer at the North British Rubber Company. Mother, Efffie, short for Euphamia, was a cleaning lady.

Thomas started helping with the family finances from an early age. At eight, he got a pre-school job working on the horse and carts delivering milk to homes in the rough, working-class tenements. He would also deliver newspapers and work at a butcher's shop. School took a back seat to earning money, as well as a growing obsession with football and Saturday mornings spent at the cinema. He was a big fan of the Three Stooges, Flash Gordon, and the cowboy flicks. By 14, Connery had quit school altogether. 'The war was on, so my whole education time was a wipe out,' he said. Around the same time, he lost his virginity to an older woman in an Auxiliary Territorial Service (ATS) uniform.

That lack of an education would bother him in later years, especially when he started mixing in theatre and film circles, with actors and writers from a different class, many of whom had gone to university. Nevertheless, what he had learned in those early years was a fierce independence and a strong sense of self-reliance. There would also be an obsession with money which some observers would characterise as greed. It wasn't. It was more a determination to make sure he was paid every penny that he thought he was worth, and that he was owed. These were traits that future producers and studios would have to learn to abide by. He had a schoolyard friend called Seamus who he always hung out with, and they became known as Seamus and Shane, which would late migrate into Sean. Although, as he grew taller and developed his muscular frame, most people called him 'Big Tam'.

As a teenager, he was giving Effie, £2 10 shillings a week from his multiple jobs to help support the family. He would do that for a couple more years, but 'Big Tam' already knew there was no real future for him in this succession of low paid, manual jobs, or in the overcrowded tenement flat he shared with his parents and younger brother Neil.

At 17, he defied Joe and Effie and ran off to join the navy, signing up for seven years active service. If Sean figured a life at sea would be the making of him, he would soon realise the error of his thinking. He did a bit of boxing but overall hated the strict regime of military life which was as suffocating as his parent's Fountainbridge flat. After developing stomach pains, he was diagnosed with a duodenal ulcer and discharged on medical grounds. The only legacies from his short naval career were a disability pension of 6s 8d a week and two tattoos. One said, 'Mum and Dad' and the other, 'Scotland Forever'.

Now he was back where he started, living with his parents, uneducated, no qualifications and little in the way of prospects. He got back into civvy work as an odd job man, bouncer, cement mixer, steel bender, pool lifeguard and road worker for the Corporation. Theatre had played no part in Sean's childhood. A casual job, helping backstage at the Kings Head Theatre in the city, gave him his first taste of showbusiness and he began by stripping off and modelling for art students.

'You posed for 45 minutes,' remembered Sean. 'It wasn't nude. You wore a pouch thing, but that was it. It was very arduous, quite a good discipline.'

Working-class Edinburgh was a tough place to live and Big Tam would have to defend himself against gangs and would-be gangsters. But he was more than capable of beating the respect out of them. One local gang leader decided he liked the leather coat that Sean wore and wanted it for himself. His team of hoods jumped Big Tam and, one by one, he laid them out. There were offers from local crews for him to join them, but for all his muscle and capacity with his fists, Connery had no interest in becoming just another street thug.

As an ex-sailor, he got a place on a course run by the British Legion, training to be a French polisher. That led to a stint polishing coffins, but the job didn't last long. Next he got employment in a newspaper printing press. It was a decent, steady job with a future that looked as if it might be his career, and life, going forward.

Around the same time he took up bodybuilding at a local gym, working on the physique that had been formed by his early years of manual labour. With a mate, he decided to travel down to London and try out for a Mr Universe competition. Up in Edinburgh, Big Tam would have seemed like a natural for the contest. He was 6ft 2in tall, muscular, and handsome. But in London, he was up against American bodybuilders who took the discipline of developing defined, bulging muscle to a whole new level. Big Tam was disappointed to come third in the tall man division of the contest. And that would have likely been that if another competitor hadn't told him about a touring production of the musical *South Pacific*.

141

They were looking for well built, handsome guys for the chorus line.

Sean Connery auditioned and got picked. His acting career had begun. And it might also have ended there. He joined the South Pacific XI football team who played matches against local sides as they toured the country. Manchester United's legendary manager Matt Busby happened to be watching one such match from the sidelines, scouting for new talent. He was impressed by the tall Scotsman and approached Sean after the match, offering him a contract for £25 a week.

It was a temptation for the soccer mad Sean but he knew a top-class footballer's career could easily be over by 30, and he was already 23. He turned Busby down. Big Tam was starting to think seriously about a career as an actor and he figured that might be a better bet for a long-term career. 'I decided to become an actor,' he said, years later. 'And it turned out to be one of my more intelligent moves.'

As the tour progressed, Sean got promoted out of the chorus line and into roles that involved actual dialogue. A fellow actor encouraged Sean in his new ambition, recommending plays and classic literature for him to read. He was 23 years old and the education he missed out on as a child was about to commence. 'I spent all the time on the tour going to the library in whichever town we were in,' he remembered. 'Because one was always staying in pretty lousy digs, you know, so it was the theatre and the library. I had a motorcycle with me, so I'd usually go to the theatre in the morning to collect the mail and whatever I needed, and then go from there to the library or the repertory or the cinema in the afternoon. And that's how I turned it all around and gave myself an education.'

Connery got himself a cheap tape recorder and used it to work on his diction and soften that thick Edinburgh accent. After 18 months touring the country, he moved to London set on a proper acting career. He started picking up small roles in stage plays.

His first screen appearance was a walk on part in *Lilacs in the Spring*, a best forgotten British musical starring Anna Neagle and Errol Flynn. The film was a commercial and critical failure. And nobody much noticed Sean. He went through the usual rites of passage for struggling young actors. As he was frequently out of work, the experience of the austerity and poverty of his childhood served him well. Sean would go to the butcher, bargain for the cheapest cuts of meat and produce a big pot of stew that would keep him going for a few days.

He became a regular at the Buckstone club, a small meeting place for actors and film and theatre people in London's West End. He would be hanging out with the likes of Peter Finch and Stanley Baker, making a half pint of beer last all night. He played a small-time crook in an episode of the long running British TV police drama, *Dixon of Dock Green*. It would be just one of a frustrating run of minor roles in mostly forgettable television shows and films, usually playing villains, thugs, bouncers; roles that gave him no chance to stretch.

'I did some useful things on stage and TV.' He remembered. 'Then I did the rounds, and I was either too tall, too fat, too thin, too Scottish, too handsome, too ugly. One geezer said I looked too Polish!' Sean got his first substantial role in a film, playing a criminal with a speech impediment in *No Road Back*. But it was in television where he finally got a part that, while still exploiting his physicality, offered him a chance to actually act.

The BBC, responding to the new competition from the launch of a rival channel, Independent Television, was looking to up its drama output. The American actor Jack

Palance had won plaudits for his performance as a punch-drunk boxer in the drama, *Requiem for a Heavyweight*, broadcast live on American television. The BBC's plan was to bring Palance over to revisit his role in a live broadcast of the play for a British audience, but a few weeks before the planned broadcast, Palance backed out.

A replacement was needed urgently, and Sean Connery got the call. It was a nerve-racking enterprise. There were no opportunities for errors or re-takes when you are broadcasting a play live to the nation. The play got mixed reviews, but Connery acquitted himself well. The review *The Times* said: 'Although physically miscast as the fighter, Mr. Sean Connery played with a shambling and inarticulate charm that almost made the love affair credible.'

Finally, he was being recognised for his acting skills. He continued studying, reading his way through the classics, taking acting classes, absorbing knowledge from any source, like a sponge. It was all in service of a class fuelled ambition to prove himself, not only as an actor, but as an intelligent, well-rounded man, and not some uneducated bouncer from the slums of Edinburgh.

The actor James Fox, who came from the sort of privileged background that was as far removed from Connery's as it was possible to be, got to know him well. 'He rather despised the privilege system in our country,' said Fox. 'But battled on to show his contemporaries who is the real star.' Sean was never short of female company, and he now had a regular girlfriend, an accomplished actress named Diane Cilento. Diane also came from a different place. She was born in Australia, schooled in New York, and accepted into RADA in London. She was well-educated, and much more at ease amongst the brilliant minds and wits of London's creative hub. When they started dating, she was still married, and separated, from an Italian aristocrat and had a small child. Her first opinion of Sean was that: 'He looked fun but dangerous.'

Diane was intelligent, highly educated, sophisticated and talented. She would go on to be nominated for an Oscar for the British film *Tom Jones*, made by Saltzman's former cohorts at Windfall Films. Right now, she was another source of education for him. Her take on Connery was slightly different from that of Fox. She said, 'he had a terrific chip on his shoulder'.

Sean was cast in a minor role in *Action of the Tiger*, the ill-fated movie in which the director, Terence Young, had advised him to 'keep swimming'. A year later, America came calling. When 20th Century Fox offered a seven-year contract, that wide streak of independence Sean had developed as a child came to the fore. Did he really want to sign himself into a multi-year contract with a studio, even if it were a major Hollywood studio? Instinctively he rebelled against the very notion of locking himself into a long contract. But his equally fierce ambition kicked in and won the day. *Another Time. Another Place* would not be the start of major things. If the failure of the film was a blow for Sean, so then were the stream of roles and movies he was subsequently offered by the studio. None of them interested him and he doggedly refused them all. He had allowed himself to sign away his freedom for a studio contract and it was all for nothing. It would be the last time he would tie himself into a contract to one studio.

Instead of hanging around waiting for 20th Century Fox to hand him a role he thought worthy of his talents, Sean turned back to television and the stage. At least here he was now respected enough as an actor to be offered challenging parts. Just as importantly the work provided fresh opportunities to learn. He played John Proctor in a BBC version of Arthur Miller's *The Crucible*. He took on the role of Count Vronsky opposite Claire Bloom in *Anna Karenina*. He travelled to Canada to play the lead in *Macbeth* on the stage. The BBC decided to film a mammoth adaptation of 15 hours of Shakespeare's historical plays. Connery played Hotspur in *Henry IV, Part 1*. He used his own accent at a time when Shakespeare in Britain was still usually performed with RP accents.

He had met Diane when they both starred in a production of Eugene O'Neill's *Anna Christie* at the Oxford Playhouse. He and Diane performed together again in a stage production of Luigi Pirandello's *Naked*, which she had translated from the Italian. He would later take on the lead role in a Terence Rattigan play about Alexander The Great on the BBC. 'Sean Connery played Alexander as a direct and lusty soldier to the hilt,' according to *The Stage* newspaper's review. *The Times*' critic compared his performance to 'a young (Laurence) Olivier'.

In 1959 he was rejected after auditioning for *The World of Paul Stickley*, a musical satire from the 'angry young man' John Osborne. It would prove a lucky escape. After the stage triumphs of *Look Back in Anger* and *The Entertainer*, Osborne's musical was a critical and commercial failure, with one critic calling it as 'pure spit and vomit thrown directly into the teeth of the audience'.

This was all a long way away from Hollywood glamour, but then Sean Connery was never in the business for glamour. 'There's nothing special about being an actor,' he once remarked. 'It's a job like being a bricklayer and I've never stopped being amazed at the mystique people attach to my business.'

Instead of tailored suits, he bought his clothes from dirt cheap army surplus stores. He spent his free time doing all the work; plastering, cementing, carpentry, fixing up the rundown house he had bought in London. He discovered a new sport to get passionate about. A friend had introduced him to golf, which was the perfect pastime for a jobbing actor who spends a major part of their day hanging around, waiting to be offered work.

Ken Adam, a set designer who would become an integral part of the production team for the Bond films, had got to know Sean from the loose assembly of film and theatre folk at the Buckstone Club. 'He was a black and white character,' said Adam. 'Black was black and white was white. There were no greys. That was what appealed to me about Sean. In a way there was no sophistication. He was very straight in his viewpoints and very honest in what he had to say about anything to anyone.

'There was nothing superficial about him. He was incredibly good looking and very much a man's man. He was obviously very successful with women, but I think he felt more at home in a man's environment.'

Sean did manage to make a few cinema films during this time. 20th Century Fox, tired of paying their contracted actor to sit at home or do theatre, loaned him to Disney for a whimsical little film they were making about leprechauns and stolen pots of gold. Although set in Ireland, it was all shot on the back lots in Hollywood. The film was light, breezy family fare. Sean got to sing a duet with Janet Munro, his romantic lead. The former chorus line boy from the provincial tour of South Pacific who couldn't sing a note would soon have a record out. Walt Disney himself visited the set and had taken a fatherly interest in the young actor.

Sean found the experience of making *Darby O'Gill* an enjoyable one. Apart from one jarring note. Connery had not talked much about the incident involving Stompanato on the set of *Another Time, Another Place*. He was too much of a gentleman to brag about stuff like that. However, following the mobster's death, stories about the Pinewood incident had got out and made its way back to Stompanato's connected friends and they were not happy about it. While making *Darby O'Gill*, Sean received a threatening message left him at the Hollywood Roosevelt Hotel where he was staying. It was sent down from Mickey Cohen. It was like a scene from one of the B-list crime movies Sean was trying to avoid.

He immediately packed his bags and moved into an anonymous motel in the San Fernando Valley for the remainder of the Disney shoot. He might have imagined he had left the violent hoods back in Fountainbridge, but it seemed like they turned up everywhere. When it was release, the family film was a success with audiences. Eventually 20th Century Fox, tired of paying their actor to not make films with them, released him early from his contract.

There were other screen roles. *On The Fiddle* was a small British comedy about a pair of dodgy soldiers trying to line their own pockets when there was a war on. Sean played the supporting role to the film's main star, Alfred Lynch. After the world went crazy for Bond, *On The Fiddle* would get an American release, retitled *Operation Snafu*. The new name, as well as the accompanying advertising campaign, downplayed the film's comic elements and tried to pitch it as a thriller.

Sean signed on for a small role in *The Longest Day*, an ambitiously epic war drama telling the story of D-Day from the viewpoint of both the Allies and the Germans. The stellar cast included Henry Fonda, Edmond O'Brien, Rod Steiger, John Wayne, Richard Burton, Robert Mitchum, Robert Ryan, George Segal and Richard Todd. Connery had to request that the filmmakers shoot his couple of scenes early as he needed to head off to Jamaica to start location filming on his next film.

NO ONE WOULD REMEMBER COLUMBUS

When Cubby Broccoli called Sean about the Bond role, that unhappy relationship with 20th Century Fox was playing on his mind. He had tied himself to a studio thinking it would be a good career move and it had caused him nothing but frustration. While Broccoli and his producer partner Harry Saltzman were not a studio, he knew they would be looking to lock in an actor to return to the Bond role if the first film was successful.

Sean had been managing his career quite well as an independent talent. He scored some impressive roles in television and on stage and appeared in few films where he had enjoyed the process and was proud of the finished product. He had come from nothing, knowing no one in the business, but he had worked hard, studied and grafted and earned his dues as a working actor. One of the most irritating things about the stardom that would come with playing Bond was the reporters and the newspapers who would constantly refer to him as a newcomer, as if Cubby Broccoli had wandered into a pub, saw Sean propping up the bar, sipping a pint, and decided to make him a star. 'If America had been discovered as many times as I have,' said Connery, 'No one would remember Columbus'.

10 A bit of veneer over that tough Scottish hide

Before the war, Terence Young hung out with a smart set of London's café society elite. Bright young things from good families with money, confidence, and a sense of entitlement. There was one character on the fringes of this group that didn't quite belong. His was an extraordinary story and he would go on to have an even more extraordinary wartime career. If any would-be Ian Fleming attempted to invent a fictional character like Eddie Chapman, it's unlikely a publisher would find the story credible enough to publish.

Chapman was born into modest circumstances in County Durham. His father was a former marine engineer turned publican. Eddie was a bright child but had a serious discipline problem and often played truant from school. He joined the Coldstream Guards but soon realised that life in a uniform was not a good fit for him. He went AWOL with a girl he met in Soho, but when the army finally caught up with him, Chapman was thrown into military prison and then dishonourably discharged.

Back in civvy life, he drifted in petty crime, fraud and thieving before moving up the criminal career ladder to become a safecracker. He seemed to cheerfully accept that his chosen vocation would necessarily involve regular stints in prison. Despite his devotion to a life outside the law, he was proud that he had never physically hurt anyone. Eddie Chapman was not that class of criminal. He was also a very generous crook. When things were going his way, he was as adapt at spending money as he was at stealing it.

Chapman found his tribe in Soho, hanging out with a motley, bohemian crowd that inhabited this corner of London; louche actors, alcoholic writers, shady journalists; aristocratic playboys slumming it alongside criminals and prostitutes. It also attracted a glamourous set. Eddie would enjoy the company of Noël Coward, Marlene Dietrich and Ivor Novello, and he struck up a friendship with a stylish young man about town, Terence Young.

Young, born in Shanghai, educated at Harrow School and fresh out of Cambridge, was carving out a career as a screen writer. He was also busy cutting a dashing figure around town. He was tall, handsome, athletic, and always dressed impeccably in tailored suits. A driver of fast cars, and with a string of beautiful young women on his arm. Young found Chapman intriguing. 'He was able to talk on almost any subject. Most of us knew he was a crook, but nevertheless we liked him for his manner and personality.' When war broke out, Eddie was, at the time, locked up a prison cell in the Channel Islands. And he was still locked up there when the Germans invaded the islands and took control of the territory. Chapman offered himself up to the Nazis as a possible spy working for them back in Britain.

It was an extraordinary proposition, but they took him up on the offer. They flew him to mainland Europe, and he was trained in espionage, radio operation and high explosives. Then they parachuted him back into England in the dead of night with a suitcase of gelignite, £1,000 in cash and a cyanide capsule. His mission was to carry out acts of sabotage in support of the German war effort. Once back in his homeland, Chapman walked into a police

151

station and gave himself up. He then offered his services to MI5. The officers of the miliary intelligence agency were obviously suspicious. A convicted safebreaker with a lengthy criminal record who had been busted out of gaol by the Nazis wasn't the best resume. However, reluctantly, they agreed to work with him.

And so, Chapmen spent the rest of the war operating as a bizarre double, or perhaps more correctly a triple, agent, travelling between Allied and enemy territories, carrying false information to the Nazis and gaining their confidence so he could then provide intelligence to his bosses in London. To maintain his credibility with the Germans, Eddie and MI5 agents cooked up a pretend sabotage attack on an aircraft factory in Hatfield. The false damage, which Eddie would tell his Nazi handlers was down to him, was mocked up on the site. The 'damage' was convincing enough when it was photographed by German reconnaissance planes flying high above the clouds. For good measure, MI5 planted a story about the attack in the *Daily Express*.

On one side of the war, Chapman had the Germans pinning medals on his chest for what they believed were his determined efforts to help them to victory. Meanwhile he continued providing information to the British secret services. He managed to extend the subterfuge to his love life as well. At one point, he had two fiancés, one living on each side of a divided Europe. 'He is a crook and will always be one,' Young told a lawyer friend about Chapman. 'But he probably has more principles and honesty of character than either of us.'

In the 1930s Chapman had been so taken with his dapper new friend, he started acquiring some of Young's stylish elan. He bought his suits in Saville Row and acquired a flashy set of wheels. He had a table reserved at The Nest, a fashionable joint in Kingly Street in his beloved Soho, where he held court with his famous and infamous friends and many young women.

Shift forward thirty years. When Terence Young heard that his new producer bosses, Broccoli and Saltzman, were determined to sign Connery for the Bond role, he put his head in his hands and predicted: 'Disaster, disaster, disaster.'

He was sceptical of Cubby's assertion that Connery would be perfect to play the part if they could just put 'a bit of veneer over that tough Scottish hide'. But that was the task now facing the director. However, if the example of Young's lifestyle could assist an incorrigible crook like Eddie Chapman in passing himself off in high society, then maybe Young could perform the same trickery with Connery.

The director had worked with the actor before on the unremarkable *Action of the Tiger*, where he had advised Sean to 'keep swimming'. He genuinely liked Connery, but he had serious doubts on whether he had what it would take to convincingly pull of the suave, sophistication of Bond. All the same, that eager young bit player who had asked him 'Sir, will I be a success?' had spent the intervening years learning his craft and developing his talent.

'He knew this was a big chance, and he made no mistake about it,' said Young. 'But don't forget — he was a damned good actor by then. He'd had stage success. He'd appeared in *Macbeth*, and he'd been brilliant in a Jean Giraudoux play called *Judith*, which played in the West End for about six months. Besides, four or five years had elapsed since *Action of the Tiger*. He'd matured, he'd become a better actor, and when the chance came, he was ready for it.'

Sean Connery did not possess some of basic physical features of the James Bond as laid out in the novels.

Certainly he was tall, dark and handsome. But for one thing he was Scottish, not English. His eyes were a dark brown, and not the 'cold blue eyes' that suggested anger and cruelty. They both had naval careers of course. However, Sean's brief period as an ordinary seaman, pensioned offer with an ulcer, did not compare to Bond's status as a Commander of the Royal Navy. There was also the small matter of his receding hairline. Connery had been worried about hereditary hair loss since his teens and now hitting his thirties, it was noticeably disappearing. He had been named Thomas after his paternal grandfather, although grandad had been more commonly known around Edinburgh as 'Baldie Connery'.

In reality, the director and his producers were less concerned about their actor having the superficial similarities to their fictional hero. What was much more critical, if this film were to succeed, was for Connery to inhabit the character of the man. 'I had a very clear idea of what an old Etonian should be,' said Young. 'I was a guards officer during the war, and I thought I knew how Bond should behave.'

'I think the most important element in the whole series, apart from Fleming himself, was Terence Young,' Connery would say much later. 'I think he was the greatest influence. Terence had really identified, very much, with being the grand seigneur. He took me on the trip to get our clothes and everything and it was an eye-opener.'

Connery's life story may have been far removed from that of his character but what they did share was focus and fortitude. What the sceptics like Fleming could not see when they looked at Connery was how driven this man was by a determination to succeed. And while Connery could be arrogant and pig-headed, he wasn't so proud that he was incapable of taken instruction from somebody who could help his cause. 'Terence took me in hand and kicked me into shape,' he said.

Connery had worn a tux before in some of his film roles, but they would always look cheap and ill-fitting. They didn't enhance the man. Usually, they made him look like the nightclub bouncer he used to be. With the help of Young's own Saville Row tailor, they made Connery look like he was born to wear these clothes. 'I took Sean to my shirtmaker, my tailor and my shoemaker, and we filled him out,' said Terence.

There were many intense conversations about every aspect of Bond's wardrobe, from his tiepin to his wallet and his gun holster. Connery had a trilby fitted from Lock and Co of St James, and then Terence took him next door to John Lobb Bootmaker for Bond's handmade shoes. 'The budget on the clothes was astronomical in relation to the film,' said Connery, 'But he was right, Terence, because there was a look about it.'

At Young's personal tailer, Anthony Sinclair in Conduit Street, his suits were cut in the traditional way, apart from slight alterations to ensure the line of the jacket was not disrupted by Bond's gun holster under his left arm. The holster itself was specially made from soft leather and lined with blue satin to create less of a bulge.

At the bespoke shirt makers, Turnbull & Asser in Jermyn Street, Connery and Young opted for a double cuff with two buttons design for Bond's shirts, instead of cufflinks. The design is called a 'cocktail cuff' and was favoured by Young. They figured making the shirts easier to put on and off might be an asset for a bed hopping secret agent.

Bond would smoke the same cigarettes as his creator, a blend of Balkan and Turkish tobacco made specially for Fleming by the Morland tobacco shop in Grosvenor Street. Both the real author and the fictional agent had the shop put three gold bands around the width of the cigarettes. The bands donated their shared naval title of Commander. Bond carried his smokes in a wide, gun-metal cigarette case, and he lit them using a black oxidised Ronson lighter. Young next ordered his perplexed student to sleep in his new, expensive suits. The only way a true gentleman ensures his clothes fit perfectly. The actor was impressed at how, after a night's sleep in the suit, it perfectly retained its shape.

Just as importantly they talked about getting into the psyche of the character. 'I see Bond as a complete sensualist,' said Connery. 'His senses are tight and he's awake to everything. I particularly like him because he thrives on conflict, a quality lacking in present day society.'

Terence insisted on a bout of elocution lessons for Connery. The thick Edinburgh brogue had been tempered by his years as a professional actor, but the director felt it needed to be dampened down a bit more. According to set designer Ken Adam, Terence treated Sean 'like a girl at some fashionable finishing school.'

The director took Sean to the finest restaurants in London to learn how to deal with waiters. How to read a wine menu. How to order those all-important cocktails. How to light his cigarette. How to light a woman's cigarette. How to speak. How to walk across a room. At the same time he introduced Sean to Beluga Caviar and Dom Perignon and educated him on the best vintages.

Onlookers say Sean took to the training like a fish to water. He was learning which knife to use with which course, how to open an oyster, how to talk across a dinner table without disrupting the flow of the conversation.

All of these elements would help define the unique image of James Bond crafted in that first film *Dr No,* and then replicated and replayed in all the subsequent Bond films. 'There is real style in the movement of the piece,' said Sean. 'Terence Young was stamped all over it.' Young then got Connery to cut his hair and had him fitted him with two wigs to cover his rapidly balding pate. One for dry shooting on land and the other for when he was in the water. He even managed to persuade Connery to slightly trim those impressive eyebrows.

'Terence Young could have played James Bond,' said *Dr No* editor Peter Hunt. 'It was his style and his schooling of Sean that really made James Bond James Bond.'

With the encouragement of his girlfriend Diane, Connery had become a regular student of Yat Malmgren, a Swedish dance and acting teacher working in London. Yat specialised in working with actors, helping them explore movement as part of their research into whatever part they were playing, and tutoring them to be more aware of how they used their bodies.

'How to use your space is the number one key priority,' said Connery of the Yat method. 'How you stand in relation to other people in scenes, how you dance with them. That's what it's all about.'

The teacher was popular with many of the young up and coming actors of the time like Anthony Hopkins and with future generations, including Tom Hardy, Colin Firth, Michael Fassbender and Pierce Brosnan. That training certainly helped Connery find his role as Bond.

Terence was maddened by the Scot's working-class habit of waving his hands around when he talked and got him to put a stop to that. 'Sean was a rough diamond at the time,' said Adam. 'I think Terence taught him everything he knew. He had an enormous influence in creating James Bond in the person of Sean.' Years later, Connery would put it simply: 'Terence should have played Bond.'

The two men shared the same sense of humour, and

both agreed on the absolute necessity of injecting some of that humour into Fleming's character. Connery, who could be as straight a talker as anyone, had even brought up the issue with the author. 'When I became involved with the films,' said Sean 'in the first instance I felt there was a lack of humour. When I raised this with Ian, when I mentioned the business of humour, he was quite surprised because he felt he was quite humorous. He was as himself, but in writing he wasn't. That was one of the things one had to do, imbue a humour aspect in a realistic basis.'

Astutely, Young also recognised that the sexual content and violence in the Bond stories would attract unwanted attention from the film censors. The addition of wry, funny asides would help to make the excesses of this cold-blooded and sexually promiscuous assassin more palatable. According to Ken Adam, with Young and Connery, it was rather like watching a 'father son relationship'. Young himself refused to take too much credit for the successful transformation of Sean into James. 'If you asked me what the three ingredients for James Bond were,' he said. 'It was Sean Connery, Sean Connery and Sean Connery.' Although he did add, modestly: 'I must say I think Sean was much better dressed in my three pictures than in any of the others.' And he is right about how crucial Connery's casting was, in certain key aspects. There were many excellent actors in London at the time who could pull off the role of a sophisticated, urbane, old Etonian spy without raising an eyelid. Indeed, many of them, like James Fox, came from a similar class and background as the author and his creation.

However, part of Connery's success in the role of Bond would be because of the disparity between the actor and his character. Thirty years earlier, Young had befriended Eddie Chapman, an unrepentant miscreant, safe cracker and habitual jailbird, and talked admiringly about his integrity. In 1961, where many people looked at Sean Connery and all they saw was an earthy, bone-headed, working-class Scot, Young saw that same core quality. 'He doesn't give a damn for the ancillary assets of being a star,' said Terence about Sean. 'It's not that he's ungrateful. It's just that he's concerned with personal integrity. A hell of a lot of people don't like Sean because of this.'

Connery was paid £6,000 for the film, which was not a great deal of money for a leading role, and certainly much less than many of the other actors who were, publicly at least, considered for the part. In this department he shared something with his director. Terence came cheaper than other directors Cubby and Harry had approached about the job. But somehow, the bargain hunting producers, having failed to attract many of their first choices of talent, had lucked into the exact perfect combination of director and actor who would translate Bond successfully and memorably onto the big screen.

Dr No's director, Terence Young, may have drawn on memories of his old friend Eddie Chapman when helping Connery create the screen Bond. Chapman had been a notorious English criminal, spy and double agent.

11 If you look the part, self-confidence will arrive

Harry Saltzman and Cubby Broccoli now have all the option rights sorted. This is despite some fresh legal entanglement involving the authorship of one of the novels they had understood to be part of their deal with Ian Fleming. They have the financing for the film in place, with studio backing from the States and distribution sorted. Agreement has been reached on which novel to adapt for this first film and they have a working script, ready to go.

Casting of the all-important leading man has taken place and been agreed by the executives at United Artists. They have appointed a director, the production crew and most of the supporting cast. Already there are some of their people on the ground in Jamaica checking out locations for the six-week shoot, employing the necessary local support staff and extras, sorting through the official paperwork and all the red tape and bureaucracy needed to accommodate a sizable film crew and cast arriving at a foreign port of call to shoot a movie.

Meanwhile, back home in Pinewood Studios, just to the west of London, another team is already at work on designing and building the sets that would be needed for the interior scenes. The casino where Bond is first introduced to cinema audiences. The panelled office of his boss 'M'; Bond's bachelor flat; the inner sanctum of Bond's antagonist and, most challenging of all, his nuclear facility. Finally, everything is ready to commence with the filming of the first 'proper' Bond movie.

The plane carrying the core of the team touches down at the Palisadoes Airport, Kingston, on 14 January 1962. Okay, so they have a director who is, at the very least, their fifth or sixth choice after the gig was turned down by all the others they approached. And the leading actor is someone neither the studio, the novels' author or the director were keen on. But he felt like the last man standing after so many of the alternatives they had considered had passed on the role.

The producers themselves are a mismatched pair, only working together through a marriage of convenience. Both come to the project with individual track records of producing more than their fair share of turkeys and box office flops. They are about to start production on a story about a fictional character which has been rejected by many of the world's top film executives and studios. Those movie professionals all said Bond was just too violent, too sexual, and too damned English to be filmable. Even their leading man can't be counted as a Bond aficionado. Before filming, Sean Connery has only read two of the novels: 'The thing was I found Fleming much more interesting than his writing,' said the actor. One of their main screenwriters has already left the production, before a single frame has been shot. He even asked for his name to be removed from the credits, as he didn't want to be associated with this 'piece of crap'.

And yes, there are some small but significant roles that still need to be filled for scenes planned in Jamaica. They don't have the budget to bring out bit part players from England. but they're sure they'll be able to pick up some

161

eager and talented amateurs in the colony to help them out. There has never been a major motion picture shot in Jamaica so there's no local experience or infrastructure they could call on. But, hell, at least they're here now, on location and about to start the production with six weeks of shooting.

It's a bit unfortunate that neither the producers nor director has actually met the leading lady of their film. Not do they have any idea if this stunningly beautiful but inexperienced actress can actually act. They'll just have to find that out when she flies in to join them on the set. For good measure, their leading man had tripped and twisted his knee on his way to the airport in London. Sean had a quick bout of first aid and limped onto the plane flying them out to their destination.

Ian Fleming recommended the producers employ the son of Blanche Blackwell, one of his closest friends on the island, as a runner and production assistant. Chris Blackwell was born in London but spent much of his childhood in Jamaica and had started his own fledgling, local record label, called Island Records, a few years earlier. His mother was a sometime lover of Fleming and, as it happens, something of a muse for the author. Blanche was said to have provided the inspiration for some of Bond's most memorable lovers, including Pussy Galore, as well as Honeychile Rider, who appears in the *Dr No* novel and will be Bond's main female of interest in the film.

Fleming figured that young Chris would be a useful contact for the crew. His family knows everyone in the expat community and Chris would be an excellent guide to the most beautiful locations as well as the best restaurants and nightclubs on the island. The author is also a big fan of the local calypso music of Jamaica and hopes Chris could convince the producers to include some of it in the film.

IF YOU LOOK THE PART, SELF-CONFIDENCE WILL ARRIVE

Blackwell will indeed prove to be an invaluable asset to the crew. So much so that after shooting was completed, Saltzman offered him a full-time job with the Eon production company. Chris considered the offer but stuck with his day job instead. He went on to build Island Records into one of the most successful independent record labels in the world, bringing Bob Marley and other reggae and ska artists to international audiences, as well as signing the likes of Roxy Music and U2.

The key villain of their film is the mysterious and reclusive Dr No, the son of a Chinese girl of good family and a German Methodist missionary. Like future Bond villains, Dr Julius No is physically impaired. He is exceptionally tall and wears metal claws for hands. As Dr No explains to Bond over dinner and a bottle of Dom Perignon '55, he had once been a member of the Tong, a criminal syndicate in China. When they found out he was embezzling from them, they cut off his hands as punishment. Now, left with hooks for hands, he has reinvented himself as Dr Julius No: 'Julius for my father, no for my rejection of him'

The screenwriters had thought *Dr No* a dreadfully old fashioned and out of date villain for a modern Sixties thriller. 'Fu Manchu with claws for hands,' as one of the writers, Richard Maibaum, described him. But the producers had vetoed their attempts to radically meddle with the character. The big adjustment of *Dr No* from the novel to the screen was to replace his hooks with solid metal hands. On behalf of the producers, Fleming had approached his friend, and Jamaican neighbour, Noël Coward to see if he would be interested in playing the baddie. Coward replied by telegram: 'Dr No? No, No, No.'

Fleming's other suggestion for the role was his stepcousin, Christopher Lee. Lee made his screen debut in Terence Young's first picture as a director, Corridor of

Mirrors, and since made a name for himself as a stalwart of the Gothic horror movies over at Hammer Films. In the end, the producers went with Joseph Wiseman, a Canadian American actor best known for his work in the theatre on Broadway. Wiseman accepted the role little imagining it would be the thing he would go on to be best remembered for: 'I had no idea it would achieve the success it did. As far as I was concerned, I thought it might just be another grade-B Charlie Chan mystery.'

Wiseman would deliver a performance marked by a still, calm menace, which would become a template for the future Bond villains on screen. His character, rather helpfully, explains his evil scheme to the secret agent, which would be another trait for future Bond villains to adopt. And Christopher Lee would just have to wait another decade, until *The Man with the Golden Gun*, to get his opportunity to play a Bond baddie.

Dr No's reclusive enclave on Crab Key is home to a flock of rare birds. This provides a respectable front: selling of the birds' deposits of guano as fertilizer. The adventure is set off by reports that a group of ornithologists from the National Audubon Society had visited the island to study the birds. They have since gone missing. As Bond would discover, the evil Dr No was responsible for their deaths, and he is using his secretive fortress on the island to sabotage US missile launches from Cape Canaveral.

One major deviation from the novel to the script is the removal of the Soviets as Dr No's allies in his endeavours. James Bond is often seen as a warrior of the Cold War. And, certainly, he's a defender of Western democracy, often working in cahoots with American counterparts, supporting its global interests and battling the same adversaries. That was certainly the Fleming version of 007.

In the films, however, there will be remarkably little

conflict that relies on the Soviets as the enemies. That was a conscious decision taken by Broccoli and Saltzman. The anti-Soviet storylines would likely go down well with audiences in America, but they were making films that they wanted to play to a global audience. It was possible some of the more sophisticated European cinemagoers would be less inclined to relish out-and-out Commie bashing on screen.

If the producers had hoped the Kremlin would be appreciative of the change in direction, they were going to be disappointed. A Soviet journalist, writing in 1965 after the Bond movie franchise had been established, described their hero in this way: 'Bond's job is to guard the interests of the property class, and he is no better than the youths Hitler boasted he would bring up like wild beasts to be able to kill without thinking.'

Instead of the Russians, Dr No was now working in tandem with a secret international criminal organisation known as SPECTRE, made up of German Nazis, Italian Mafia, former Soviet agents and assorted criminal gangs and criminals from around the world. Their aim is global domination and to be the third player in the Cold War, often looking to find ways to pit the Americans and the Russians against each other.

SPECTRE, which stands for Special Executive for Counter-intelligence, Terrorism, Revenge and Extortion, did not appear in the novel of *Dr No*. It actually made its debut in Fleming's most recent book, *Thunderball*, which had been put together by Fleming using material in a script written by a young Irish scriptwriter and director Kevin McCrory and a fellow writer, Jack Whittingham. This is the book that is currently the subject of bitter litigation. SPECTRE gets just a minor name check in *Dr No*. The producers figure the organisation will feature more prominently in future Bond films. If there *are* future Bond films of course.

The location shoot is proving to be successful if at times, maddingly frustrating. The producers are pleased with how Sean Connery is performing in the central role. The research and homework he did with director Terence Young before they left London seems to have prepared him well for the part.

On the set, Sean is just another one of the team. He eats with the crew and can walk around the island unrecognised and unmolested. After each day's shooting he joins the extras and camera guys in the local restaurants and bars. Nobody is treating him like a film star and there are few on the set who are predicting that *Dr No* would be the film that would elevate him up onto that pedestal.

On the location shoots of future Bond films, it will be a different story. The producers will be forced to hire teams of bodyguards to keep the set clear of fans and media. Connery will not be able to walk more than a few yards without being mobbed. By the time they are shooting *You Only Live Twice* in Japan, the Paparazzi will even try to snap him in the privacy of his bathroom. But right now, he's just one of the lads. He's popular on the set, laughing and mixing easily with the technicians and the other actors, no matter how low down the bill they are.

Nevertheless, Sean does get a few opportunities to enjoy the high life. He dines with Ian Fleming, who is at his Goldeneye retreat, as well as visiting and hanging out at the neighbouring home of Noël Coward. Sean gets a particular kick out of seeing the actor-writer holding court in full Coward mode, donning a smoking jacket, cigarette holder in mouth, sitting at the piano regaling his guests with songs and quips.

The pair have struck up an unlikely friendship. For all his

upper bracket friends and affectations Coward, the son of a piano salesman and a landlady, came from a far humbler background, albeit one a few steps up the British class ladder from Connery's tough Fountainbridge childhood. Coward offered up advice on acting and Connery, ever the sponge, listened and learned. He also gave the young Scot some guidance on dealing with the press which, following the premiere of *Dr No* and his new status as a movie star, would be useful information. They discussed the character of Bond who Coward describes as a 'snob', which at least fits well with Sean's opinion of his creator.

The crew and their film are not welcomed everywhere on the island. When James Bond first arrives in Jamaica, he heads directly to King's House, the official residence of the Governor of Jamaica. At the time of filming, Jamaica was still a British colony. It would get its independence in a few short months.

Fleming had written to the current Governor about the filming of *Dr No* and asked about the possibility of using King's House as a location on the shoot. The answer is an emphatic no.

Filming on the island commenced Monday 16 January. The first scene the crew shoot is Scene 39 in the script, back at what was then named the Palisadoes Airport, Jamaica's main international airport. Bond arrives on the island to commence his mission, which is finding out who murdered John Strangeways, the island's MI6 representative.

As he makes his ways out of the terminal, he is photographed by a beautiful, female press photographer, Annabel Chung, who's secretly in the service of Dr No. The photographer is played by Marguerite LeWars, a former Miss Jamaica whose day job was working as an air hostess. Marguerite has zero acting experience and got the role after she had been spotted by Terence Young, when he arrived at the airport to scout locations and find local talent to fill out the minor roles.

Marguerite said she was on the desk, checking tickets and visas, when Terence approached her: 'He said 'would you like to be in the movies?" It took a while for him to explain why he was asking and convince her that he was genuine. Initially he wanted her to play the more significant role of Miss Taro, another Dr No agent, who seduces Bond while trying to kill him. Marguerite told him in no circumstances could she play this part: 'I cannot lie there in a towel on a bed, kissing a strange man. My parents would object.'

She was cast in a smaller part, playing this other Dr No agent. As she snaps Bond and then watches him pass her by and depart the airport, Young instructed Marguerite to lick the camera's flashbulb, a bizarre move that she found mystifying. Perhaps if she had realised Young was looking at a way to charge her character with a perverse, sexual tension she might have thought twice.

Not surprisingly for an absolute beginner, Marguerite was struggling with her minor but crucial role. Young got more and more frustrated at her for fluffing yet another take which, in turn, made her even more nervous. The director finally called for a coffee break. It was Connery who came to the rescue, offering some sage advice. And perhaps revealing something of his own method to overcoming personal doubts in his abilities. Marguerite said: 'Sean looked at me and he said to me in his lovely Scots accent, he said "Marguerite, where is your self-confidence?" and I said: "I don't have any" and I started to cry "I'm not an actress, I want to go home".'

'He said: "Let me tell you about self-confidence. If you physically look the part, you are efficient and you project that personality, self-confidence will happen."

IF YOU LOOK THE PART, SELF-CONFIDENCE WILL ARRIVE

Her recruitment would not be the only last-minute, make do casting in the film. *Dr No* opens with three — apparently blind — street beggars making their way to their designated task: the assassination of the Station Chief John Strangeways. Strangways was played by Timothy Moxon, an English ex-actor who was living in Jamaica and operating as a crop duster. He got the role after a chance meeting in the lobby of a Kingston hotel with Young, who remembered him from his theatre days in London. One of the 'blind' assassins sent to kill him was Moxon's real-life dentist. For decades after, Moxon would be signing autographs as the actor to speak the first line of dialogue in a Bond film, as well as be the first character murdered in a Bond film.

After the assassination of Strangeways, the killers drive in a hearse to his residence where his secretary is about to call the MI6 headquarters in London. The residence used was the private house of another wealthy incomer, an American, Delores Keator. In exchange for allowing the cameras and crew to film in her home, Delores got to join the cast, briefly, playing Strangeway's secretary who is next to be murdered by the trio of assassins. After Bond's arrival at the airport, a chauffeur, Mr Jones, approaches and says he is there to take him to King's House. Mr Jones is played by Reggie Carter, the brother-in-law of Marguerite and then one of Jamaica's best-known actors.

A suspicious Bond figures out his driver is not who he says he is, and they have a fight by the side of the road. The production's stunt coordinator and stuntman Bob Simmons choreographed a realistic looking punch up between the two men, with Bond finally gaining the upper hand. But when James tries to interrogate his would-be assassin, Mr James kills himself using a poisoned cigarette. Bond props his corpse up in the back seat of the car and continues the drive up to front entrance of the property standing in for King's House. Once there he hops out and says to policeman on duty as he passes: 'Sergeant, make sure he doesn't get away.'

It's an ad lib cooked up by Connery on the spot. It stays in the film on the directions of an approving Terence Young. Throughout the shoot, he encourages his star to deviate from the script, especially if he can find ways to inject some fun and humour into Bond.

'Terence agreed with me that it would be right to give it another flavour,' said Connery, 'Another dimension, by injecting humour. But at the same time to play it absolutely straight, and realistically.'

Terence wasn't simply looking for laughs in Fleming's dry, humourless hero for laughter's sake. According to the Production Code of Motion Picture Association of America, which was still in existence but becoming more and more irrelevant to filmmakers: 'No picture shall be produced that lowers the moral standards of those who see it.'

Terence said: 'A lot of things in this film, the sex, and violence, and so on, if played straight, would be objectionable, and we're never going to get past the censors. But the moment you take the mickey out of it, put the tongue in the cheek, it seems to disarm.'

So, Terence would have Bond perform some act of brutality, a cold-blooded murder, a graphic punch up, but then have him puncture the tension of this violent scene by following it with a dry, caustic aside, which somehow, for the censors at least, served to lessen the cruelty. It would not solve all their problems with getting the films through the official controls in countries and territories around the world, but it certainly helped.

The actress Zena Marshall was cast as Miss Taro. a

IF YOU LOOK THE PART, SELF-CONFIDENCE WILL ARRIVE

Eurasian double agent working as a secretary in King's House, but also in the pay of Dr No. Young, and the team, had screen-tested around thirty Asian actresses but could not find the right girl. Zena, born in Kenya, to parents with a mixed heritage of Irish, English and French, would need extensive make up applied to create her character's Eurasian look. It is the kind of 'yellowface' casting that would cause a storm of protest today. Marshall would have the distinction of being the first screen actress to bed Bond, as well as to then go on to try and kill him.

The most challenging part of the role for this well-mannered Catholic girl was having to spit in Connery's face. Zena spent days in bed with Sean Connery but when she finally saw the film, found that much of their screen time together had been cut because of fear of the censors. Young took to filming several scenes twice for different markets. He needed to take care. If they ended up with an adult only certificate, like the Saltzman production of *Look Back in Anger*, that would spell box office poison for Bond.

The previous year, Cubby Broccoli had been one of the backers of a stage production created by the English composer Monty Norman. Monty had been working with Wolf Mankowitz on *Belle*, a musical about the life and times of the murderous Doctor Crippen. Wolf, of course, was a scriptwriter on *Dr No* before excusing himself from the project. Cubby was an enthusiastic backer of the show, which only lasted seven weeks in the West End. Monty and his musical were ahead of their times. Theatreland was not yet ready for a musical with such a macabre storyline. But it soon would be, with the successes of *Sweeney Todd* and *Phantom of the Opera*.

In London, Cubby invited Monty to a meeting with him and his new co-producer Harry to discuss music for a film they were working on. At the time, Monty had barely heard of this Bond character and, anyway, he was busy working on two new stage musicals. He was about to politely excuse himself when Harry sweetened the deal. They were going to be shooting on location in Jamaica and would Monty and his wife like to come out and join them? On the company's expenses, of course. Monty said: 'I thought, "well, I'll have some money in the bank and, if the film is a flop, at least we'll have had some sun, sea and sand".' It would be another fortuitous break in the production of the film.

The producers needed a big, bold theme song. Monty remembered a tune called *Bad Sign, Good Sign*, which he had written for another stage musical, *A House for Mr Biswas*, based on the novel by V.S. Naipaul. That project got shelved, but Monty figured the song might have a future. The original tune was conceived with an Indian musical arrangement using traditional Indian instruments. Monty figured that, with a bit of reworking and a new arrangement, it might fit the film producers' requirements.

Just as Fleming had hoped, the local calypso music made it onto the soundtrack for *Dr No*. Chris Blackwell introduced Monty and the producers to the extremely popular local band, Byron Lee and the Dragonaires, who would feature in a club scene in the film. The song Monty recorded with the band, Jump Up, would be a minor hit. The composer was able to arrange and record other calypso flavoured tunes which would become part of the soundtrack, including, for that opening scene with the assassins, a jaunty version of *Three Blind Mice*.

Ursula Andress, the woman set to play the critical role of Honey, joined the production on location. In the novel, Honeychile was described as looking not unlike Botticelli's Venus. That possibly wasn't very helpful for the casting, Back in London, Cubby and his wife Dana were watching a television play and spotted what they thought would be the perfect candidate for the role, a stunningly attractive, young actress. However, when Julie Christie turned up to their arranged meeting. looking dishevelled and in jeans, they couldn't believe it was the same girl. In the end Julie didn't get to play Honey as she didn't have the sort of voluptuous figure they were seeking for the part. With only a few weeks to go before filming commenced, they still hadn't found their Honey.

Then Cubby came across a provocative photo of Ursula, wearing just a wet shirt, among a batch of actress publicity shots. It had been taken by her husband John Derek, the American actor, director and photographer. Cubby was decided. She would be their Venus. The Swiss born Ursula had been living and working in Rome as a children's nanny where she picked up a few minor roles in Italian films. A producer had suggested she should try her luck in Hollywood. She arrived in town and was signed up by Paramount and then by Columbia but never made any actual films for either company, mostly due to her lack of English and apparent indifference to learning it.

After briefly dating James Dean, she met and married John Derek. When she got sent the *Dr No* script, she wasn't particularly interested in the role, it seemed like a very silly movie to her. But at a dinner party at their LA home, the couple's friend Kirk Douglas took a look at the script and got excited about the part. He told her she must do it. Once on set, she gelled immediately with everyone. Broccoli had made a good call. Ursula developed an easy natural rapport with Connery, which translated onto the screen. He, in turn, was generous in helping and supporting her with what was her first, major role.

Perhaps they became too close for some people's comfort. Her husband John Derek arrived on set, unannounced, half-way through the shoot. He contented himself with hanging around on the locations, taking still photos of his beautiful young wife during breaks in shooting. At least he didn't come at Sean with a gun.

Terence Young had something of a reputation for being profligate with film budgets and an almost laissez-faire attitude about keeping to the tight schedules necessary on a production. That wasn't so much of a problem on this shoot as the issues they did face were not of his making. There were unforeseen problems involving local work practises and bouts of bad weather. There was also the late arrival of some of the actors and equipment, and damage done to a key piece of on-screen machinery. Time was their big enemy. The production simply didn't have the sort of budgetary flexibility which would allow for an extended location shoot. Some key scenes and planned location shooting had to be abandoned.

Peter Hunt, the film's editor, said: 'We had a lot of problems in production. But when you haven't got very much money, and you're making a film without any big stars, you're just making a little British film, those things matter very much.' The producers were getting nervous. Any film people who came out and visited the set were asked to report back to UA and tell them that everything was going really well. They knew that there were still detractors at the studio who were dismissive of their low-budget 'Limey spy film'.

Terence did live up to his other reputation which was to lavish hospitality on his cast and crew. He would often bring out crates of champagne and gourmet food to celebrate the close of another day's labour. 'Whenever he made money, he spent it right away,' said Ursula, about her new director. 'Whatever he got, he spent it, spent it, spent it. We had champagne, all the time. Dom Perignon.

174

Caviar. I still have a shirt of his. He gave me one because I had to stand there for hours, so he gave me a custom-made Italian shirt, a pink one I remember.'

Chris Blackwell was proving his usefulness, helping them access some of the most beautiful parts that Jamaica had to offer in terms of locations. His family connections opened doors, introducing the producers to the owners of strictly private estates. The beach at Laughing Waters was owned by another expat, Mrs Minnie Simpson, who was notoriously difficult to deal with and very strict about the privacy of her property. Thankfully for the producer team, she was a big fan of the Fleming books. The beach would be used for Honey's emergence from the water. In the novel, Honey is nude and covers her face with her hand, to conceal her broken nose. These were other alterations they had to make for the screen.

The bikini was not as ubiquitous a piece of clothing in 1962 as it is now and was still regarded as something shocking. The crew had picked up another local talent, fashion designer, Tessa Welborn, who was a relative of a barman used in the film. Welborn was employed to work on Honey's wardrobe. Originally her bikini was supposed to be in a traditional, colourful Jamaican style with palm trees and tropical flowers. That was until Ursula set to work with Tessa to create something simpler, more unique and, as it turned out, iconic. The outfit was fashioned from a British Army webbing belt. The simple design they came up with would make it easier for the actress to wear while running and during the action sequences.

The character of Honey had lived most of her life outdoors, wearing little clothing and exposed to the hot Caribbean sun. Ursula arrived off the plane with pale skin. They didn't have the luxury of waiting for her to tan up naturally. The actress had to stand completely naked in her hotel room while tanning make-up was applied to her body, top to bottom. She managed to badly scrap her leg on coral when she fell while running along the beach and more make-up had to be applied to cover the scratches.

It had been Cubby's idea for Honey to sing a simple ditty as she comes out of the sea. It was good fortune then that Monty Norman was on hand to come up with *Under The Mango Tree*. Harry Saltzman loved the tune and briefly considered using it as the film's main theme. Wisely they abandoned the idea.

When Ursula emerges from the waves, holding pieces of coral she has picked from the ocean floor, it would become one of the most memorable scenes in film history. Ursula would understand how that one scene changed her life: 'All I did was wear a bikini in *Dr No*, not even a small one, and whoosh, overnight I have made it.' Even the crew seemed to realise, on the day, that they were witnessing something very special. 'The thing that looked great, right when it was being filmed, was that scene with Ursula Andress coming out of the water,' said Blackwell. 'When that scene was done, everybody applauded.'

The crew were filming another section of the beach episode, after Bond and Honey have just met. They must run for cover as an armed motor launch, manned by Dr No's minions, comes into view, and strafes the beach with machine gunfire. The actors are on their spots and the boat steams around a bend into the camera's line, its rapid gunfire throwing up sand on the beach. This sequence, which was filmed at another beach near Falmouth, had to be reshot after a group of American sailors, alerted by the sound of gunfire, rushed to the spot to see what was going on.

This is a modestly budgeted film. So, when the sand has been kicked up and needed to be levelled out for another take, Saltzman and Broccoli grabbed shovels and joined the locally employed crew at the task. Ursula only had good memories of the shoot: 'I didn't know anything about acting and Terence and Sean were very helpful to me. The thing I remember the most was we were like a family, Sean, Terence and I.'

In the script for *Dr No*, Honey gets to reveal the backstory of her life to James. It is a luxury that will not be afforded to many of the future Bond girls. The actress met the Bond author and got on well with him: 'I remember Ian Fleming came to the set. He was a fascinating man, so full of knowledge, he was lovely man.' The admiration was mutual. In the 1963 Bond novel, *On Her Majesty's Secret Service*, he slyly name checks her: 'Irma Bunt...waved a hand towards the crowded tables around them. "A most interesting crowd, do you not find? Everybody who is anybody...that is Ursula Andress, the film star..."'

Bob Simmons had been a stunt double on several Warwick films, including *The Red Beret* and *Action of the Tiger*. He would become another member of the 'Bond family'; the regular crew people who would unite every year or 18 months, usually in some far-flung exotic location, for the next 007 film. He stood in for Connery in the opening gun barrel sequence on *Dr No* and for the opening sequences on the next two Bonds, even though he was a good six inches shorter than the actor.

Despite Simmons' availability Connery, when he was able, liked to do his own stunt work. In one scene, he had to drive a small sports car between the giant tires of a construction crane. Connery's first Bond movie was almost his last movie ever. 'He's very lucky to be alive,' remembered Young. 'We damned near killed him. When we rehearsed it, he drove about five or ten miles an hour, just to see if he could go under it, and he cleared it by about four inches. But as we were shooting it, he was coming at forty, fifty miles an hour, and he suddenly realized the car was bouncing two feet up in the air, and there he was with his head sticking out. It so happened that the last bounce came just before he reached the thing. and he went down and under — or he would've been killed.'

Connery had his own version of the incident. 'If I remember correctly, going under the crane was Cubby Broccoli's idea,' said Connery, adding dryly. 'Maybe he'd paid very heavy insurance beforehand.' Connery would most certainly be calling on the services of Simmons for another scene. The Scottish actor was terrified of spiders, which was unfortunate, because they needed a pivotal scene where a tarantula is crawling across his naked body. It was doubly unfortunate that Simmons also had a fear of spiders. In the book, the deadly creature placed in Bond's bed was a poisonous centipede. The production team figured a cinema audience were more likely to be aware that a tarantula was poisonous, and so would heighten the tension of the scene.

In some of the shots, the reflection of a sheet of glass can just be detected, shielding Connery from the arachnid, while Simmons stood in for Sean for other sections of filming the scene. The tarantula, whose name was Rosie, would have a film career beyond *Dr No*. She was in the Bob Hope film, *Call Me Bwana*, which Saltzman would go on to produce. In fact, the scene with Hope and the spider would be a comic rip-off of this sequence. Rosie would also have a small crawl on part in *Tom Jones*, the British period comedy that would win Connery's other half, Diane, her best actress Oscar nomination.

There had been much heated debate between the producers and the director over the shooting of one controversial scene. The scriptwriters had introduced a new character, not in the book, a geologist called Professor Dent. He was yet another person on the island secretly in the employ of *Dr No*. Dent was played by Anthony Dawson, who could be seen attempting to strangle Grace Kelly in Alfred Hitchcock's *Dial M For Murder*. In the story, Dent breaks into Bond's darkened bedroom at night and fires repeatedly into what he believes is the agent's sleeping body in the bed. Bond, who had been sensing a trap, had piled up the pillows under the sheets and was sitting quietly in a chair behind the door.

Several versions of the scene were written and discussed and, in the end, the toughest version, the one that risked losing the audience's sympathy for Bond, was filmed. After Dent repeatedly fires into the bed, Bond turns on the light and his would-be assassin is caught out. Dent tries to fire again but the chamber of his weapon is empty. 'That's a Smith and Western and you've had your six,' ad-libbed Connery, before shooting him in cold blood. The producers were unsure that they wanted their new screen hero to kill a man when he posed no threat to Bond or to anyone else. Would he lose the audience? But Terence Young was adamant: Bond is an executioner, and the audience should not be allowed to forget that. Sean Connery sided with his director.

'That line 'You had your six',' said Sean. 'I dreamt that up as I did in many instances in all the scripts. I had the most licence with Terence who directed the first two and the fourth. People could acknowledge and accept the violence if the scene ended upbeat.' For good measure his Bond coolly removes his silencer and blows on it. However, this would be the only time screen 007 would kill a man in cold blood.

Some of the most challenging scenes they needed to capture were when Bond, Honey and Bond's new friend,

Quarrel, traverse the inhospitable swamps and marsh lands on Dr No's Crab Key island. Quarrel was plated by John Kitzmiller, an American who served in the 92nd Infantry Division during the Italian Campaign and decided to stay on in Italy after the war ended. He starred in Italian neorealist dramas as well as other European films and was the first African American to win an award at Cannes. *Dr No* was a rare excursion into Hollywood movieland for him.

The scenes were filmed at the Vanzie Swamp, Salt Marsh, just outside of Falmouth on Jamaica. The marshes were foul and disgusting and they stank. The cast and crew had to contend with leeches and mosquitoes.

Unlike the later Bonds, the gadgetry and high-tech stuff on *Dr No* was kept to a minimum, although Bond does use a Geiger counter to check for radioactivity on Crab Key. His murderous chauffeur kills himself with a cigarette laced with cyanide and there are Dr No's prosthetic hands. In the novel, *Dr No* had created a scare story of a fire breathing dragon in the marshes to keep prying locals away from his island. In fact, it is an armoured car, manned by his henchman and fitted with flamethrowers. The crew had a tractor specially adapted in Miami, but a freak snowstorm in Florida delayed its arrival on location and it was damaged in transit. The vehicle kept breaking down or sinking into the mud during filming, delaying the production even more.

This would be the location for the death of Quarrel, caught without cover in the marshlands and burned alive by the flamethrowers. Bond and Quarrel had developed a friendship and his death would affect the normally stoic agent. This would become another part of the Bond template, a 'sacrificial lamb' would be lost. This would be someone that Bond cares about who dies during the course of the story, upping the personal stakes for 007 and allowing him to show at least a trace of human emotion.

Bond's friend and US agent Felix Leiter was imported into the *Dr No* story. Although a regular in the Bond books he makes no appearance in *Dr No*, the novel. His appearance seemed to be mainly there to give an American screen presence to the story because, frankly, the character doesn't seem to serve much other purpose in the film. This may well be because planned scenes never made it into the final cut. One such shot had Bond make a phone call to Leiter after he and Honey had been captured by Dr No. Bond was to tell the American agent that there is nothing untoward happening on Crab Key Island, in return for Dr No not torturing Honey.

Leiter is played by Jack Lord. He in no way matched Fleming's description of the character: 'a mop of straw-coloured hair lent his face a boyish look which closer examination contradicted.' But then none of the multiple actors who would fill the role in subsequent films did. Lord, who would find fame in the Hawaii Five-0 television series, had been asked to return to the role for the next Bond film. However, he apparently asked for equal billing with Connery's Bond, and more money.

The shoot had been a real family affair, with Cubby bringing his brood along, including daughter Barbara, who was only two at the time. Barbara would eventually join the family business and take up the reigns as a producer on the franchise and continue the Broccoli involvement in Bond after her father's death. The problems on location, coupled with a tight budget meant there were scenes which they would have to abandon totally or, hopefully, find a way to pick up back at Pinewood. Connery said: '*Dr No* was a very poverty-stricken production in terms of finance. It was less than the one million dollars because the dollar was devalued before we started.'

Dr No ends with the villain falling into the nuclear reactor pool of his own installation and not, as in the book, drowning in a vat of bird crap. At Reynolds Pier, a bauxite mine near Ocho Rios, they filmed the aftermath of the destruction of Dr No's hideaway, with clouds of black smoke, chaos and scores of extras paid a couple of pounds each to throw themselves into the water. Back at Pinewood, special effects guy Frank George created a model of Dr No's fortress which would be blown up for the finale and intercut with the smoke laden footage filmed at the harbour. It would be the first explosive finale of a Bond film. The first of many. The final scene became another staple trope of the franchise with Bond narrowly escaping in a small craft, with the girl. The unit packed up and left Jamaica on Friday, 23 February. Work would resume at Pinewood.

In 1956, a gun expert named Geoffrey Boothroyd wrote to Fleming. He was a big fan of the Bond books, and he had a small matter to raise with the writer. In the novels, Bond's favoured weapon was a Beretta. In Boothroyd's words, this was a 'lady's gun' and one that was likely to jam and let the agent down at key moments. He offered up suggestions for what he believed would be a more appropriate firearm for Britain's foremost secret agent. Rather than be insulted that someone would try to second guess his creative decisions, Fleming struck up a correspondence with Boothroyd and sought to exploit his expertise.

At the beginning of Fleming's next novel, *Dr No*, Bond's boss 'M' calls Bond into a meeting. They are joined by a new character, called Major Boothroyd, MI6's in-house weapons expert. 'M' commands James Bond to hand over his beloved Beretta and replace it with a German made semi-automatic Walther PPK. The scene is played out in the movie in M's plush London office. Bernard Lee plays the stern fatherly figure of 'M', castigating Bond who is returning from a period of convalesce after being injured on his last assignment. The convalescence is an oblique reference to the close of the previous Bond novel, *From Russia with Love*. In the final pages, James was attacked by Rosa Klebb, who stabbed him with a poisoned blade in her shoe and left him for dead.

Bond's new mission to Jamaica was, 'M' informed him, more of a holiday than a proper assignment. He would be looking into the murder of Strangeways. This mundane job was a form of punishment for an agent addicted to danger and adventure. Bernard Lee was pulled in to play the role of 'M' at the last minute and, according to Young, he only got the job 'because everyone else was away'. Lee would go on to portray M in the next ten Bond films. Boothroyd was played by Peter Burton. The character would be renamed Q in subsequent films. Burton was unavailable for the next film, *From Russia with Love*. and was replaced with Desmond Llewellyn, who would reprise the role in almost every Bond film until his death in 1999.

The set designer on *Dr No*, Ken Adam, had been born into an upper middle class Jewish family in Berlin. His family moved to Britain to escape the Nazis in the 1930s. He became one of only three German born pilots to fly with the RAF during the Second World War. One of the others was his brother Denis. If they had crashed and been captured, they would most likely have been put against a wall and shot for treason rather than be treated as prisoners of war. Post-war, Ken built a solid reputation as a production designer, working with directors such as Jacques Tourneur and Robert Aldrich. He had worked on three films with

Cubby and had won an award for his set designs on the final Warwick Films motion picture, *The Trial of Oscar Wilde*.

Cubby approached him about working on his next project, a low-budget British spy movie. Ken wasn't a fan of the script, and his spouse urged him not to take the job, 'My wife read it and said: "you can't possible do this. You'll prostitute yourself."' Despite his partner's reservations, Adam accepted Cubby's offer. He was given carte blanche to create the sets on the back lot at Pinewood, albeit with severely limited funds. His initial budget of £14,000 was augmented by a further £7,000 and he made the money work hard. He created a realistic rendition of Les Ambassadeurs Casino, where the audience would get their first acquaintance with Bond. The exclusive London club had played an auspicious role in the history of bringing Bond to the screen. It had been at the club where Fleming had met with Irving Allen, back when he was Cubby's business partner, and where Allen had insulted Fleming's creation as not good enough for TV. And it was here, a few short years later, where Fleming agreed to meet with Saltzman, and they first discussed the options deal that had led everyone to this place.

The character of Sylvia Trench, who meets Bond at the casino and famously gets to ask him his name, was originally planned as a recurring character in the film franchise. Eunice Gayson, who played Sylvia, said although the scene might look, on the big screen, effortless and cool, filming it was another matter. 'It sounds an easy take, but it wasn't,' said Eunice. 'It went on and on. We had problems with my dress which was the wrong colour for the set and my director was very upset. So, my dress was literally made on the spot. My red dress, which everyone was raving about, was just a piece of fabric held together with clothes pegs, because we couldn't hold up filming otherwise.'

When Bond returns to his apartment, Sylvia is there, this time dressed only in his pyjama top, playing golf on the carpet. Bond is severely tempted but he has to put his duty to country ahead of his own personal pleasure and he's off on his new assignment. Eunice had appeared in several of Young's films, and he begged her to be in this one. He told the actress: 'You are lucky to me, whenever you are in a film I direct, you are always a success.' The director had another reason for wanting her on the set. 'I knew Sean, and Terence knew that I could help him,' said Eunice. 'He was quite nervous. For years we knew, in the business, that Sean would make it big, and it hadn't happened.' But she had a clashing obligation with the film schedule, Eunice was contracted to play the Baroness in the stage version of *The Sound of Music* at the Palace Theatre in London. She had to ask permission from the theatre producers to allow her to spend the days working on the set in Pinewood. She would then jump into a helicopter and be flown into London to appear on stage at night.

The concept for her character was that, at the beginning of every subsequent film, Bond would be on a date with Sylvia and have to miss out making love, as he was called away to save the world. Eunice/Sylvia would return as the abandoned girlfriend in *From Russia with Love*, but after that the idea and the character were dropped. Instead, the humour of Bond's teasing, flirtatious relationship with M's secretary, Miss Moneypenny, would become a mainstay of the franchise. Lois Maxwell had just been dealt a devastating family blow. Her husband had suffered a double coronary and she needed to find work to support their young family. 'The doctors didn't expect him to live, and I knew I would have to find work to support us all,' said Lois. 'So, I phoned around some of the people I knew in the film business and pleaded for anything they could give me.' Terence offered her the choice of roles. She could play Miss Moneypenny or Sylvia Trench.' I didn't fancy myself just wearing a pyjama top on screen,' said Lois, 'and what's more, I'm ambidextrous, so it would almost be impossible for me to putt a ball down the corridor. So, I said I'd prefer to play Miss Moneypenny.' She received £200 for the two days of filming and had to supply her own wardrobe. It would prove to be a fortuitous decision as she would appear in fourteen Bond films in total. And, like Ursula Andress, she got the seal of approval from Fleming. After a London screening, the author approached her: 'He came up to me and said: "When I wrote the part of Miss Moneypenny I had, in my mind's eye, a tall, elegant woman with the most kissable lips in the world. You are precisely that".'

The walls of M's office and the club were made of plywood and would wobble when touched, but they looked solid enough on the screen. Although these set designs were modest compared to Adam's inspired work on Dr No's lair and nuclear facility. To assist with Adam's design planning, Saltzman had arranged for him to visit Harwell, an atomic energy research plant near Oxford. Two young scientists then came to Pinewood to guide him through the principles of a nuclear water reactor. He also managed to borrow some impressive looking computer equipment from IBM to complete the look. Adam filled Dr No's inner sanctum with beautiful, ornate furnishings. He created an impressive aquarium along one large wall, filled with 'giant fish', as a backdrop to the villain's living room.

'It wasn't a real aquarium in Dr No's apartment,' said Adam. 'It was a disaster to tell you the truth because we had so little money. We decided to use a rear projection screen and get some stock footage of fish. What we didn't realise was because we didn't have much money the only stock footage they could buy was of goldfish-sized fish. So, we had to blow up the size and put a line in the dialogue with Bond talking about the magnification.' Dr No tells an impressed Bond that his underground aquarium costs him $1 million to create, the entire budget for the film.

On Thursday 23 February, Terence Young, Cubby and Harry arrived back in Pinewood to see what Adam had been able to come up with while they were away shooting in Jamaica. Adam admitted he was nervous showing them around the sets he had constructed. If the director and his producers hated them, there was no Plan B. He'd spent his entire budget. He needn't have worried. The team burst into applause in honour of what he had achieved.

The director came back to Adam with an urgent new request. They needed a place for Professor Dent to meet with Dr No and pick up the deadly tarantula that will be planted in Bond's bedroom, but Adam had already spent his budget. 'I had to design and build that cheaply,' he said. 'I think the whole thing only cost something like £450. I came up with this stylised concept of just a bare room with this circular grilled opening in the ceiling, a chair and a table with the tarantula's cage. You just hear the disembodied voice of Dr No.' It was another inspired piece of production design. His distinctive and unique set creations, low-budget or not, would set the style and look for all future Bonds films. Adam's work on *Dr No* was so impressive that he was not available to contribute to *From Russia with Love*. He'd been stolen away by Stanley Kubrick, another American filmmaker who had set up shop in the UK, to create the sets for *Dr Strangelove*.

The scene where Bond is in the ventilation shaft was, in the novel, part of an elaborate gauntlet created by the sadistic Dr No to torture his prisoner. The ordeals included a cage of tarantulas and ended with Bond being dropped into a lagoon containing a man-eating giant squid. The scriptwriters, perhaps wisely, dropped the giant squid and cage of tarantulas and used the ventilation shaft as means by which Bond escapes his cell.

Dr No's intended fate for Honey, in the novel and in the script, was to have her about to be slowly devoured by migrating crabs. The plan had been to film this in Pinewood and a consignment of live crabs was air-transported to the studio. When the crabs arrived, however, they were frozen. Young had the idea of de-icing them with hot steam, which resulted in cooked crabs. The cast and crew got to take home crab for supper that evening. In the end, they had Bond rescue her from her chains in a flooding chamber that Ken Adam had mocked up.

Principal photography finished on Friday 30 March, after 58 days. At the post wrap party for the cast and crew, there was a minor incident that encapsulated how much England and the world were about to be changed in this new decade, and how Bond was going to be part of that change. Lois Maxwell remembers watching her co-star Ursula Andress dance with the crew. 'She was the first grown woman I had ever known who didn't wear a bra. As she danced, those wonderful breasts were just swaying. I remember thinking how marvellous it must be to be that uninhibited and I wanted to throw my bra off, but I didn't have the courage.'

When he first sat down in the edit suite to go through the rushes and start assembling the film, editor Peter Hunt was bewildered by what he was being asked to do. The cancelled production days due to foul weather and equipment breaking down, meant there were scenes, sometimes moments key to moving on the plot, which were in the script but were not there in the rushes. He also discovered that Terence Young rarely did a master shot of a scene, a standard safety feature for directors to ensure they at least had something they could use.

There were other issues with Young's idiosyncratic approach to the filming and framing of some scenes. The scene where Dr No's photographer takes Bond's photo as he arrives off the plane from London, should have been a crucial establishing shot for when Bond encounters the photographer again. But because of the way the shot is framed in the final cut, it would be easy for many in the audience to miss it. Other scenes were missing completely, leaving potential and serious gaps in the storyline. The producers' rationale was that, somehow, they could fix it all when they got back to London. So, it was now down to Hunt, in the edit suite, to ensure the footage they did shoot hung together and made sense. Thankfully Young had a clear notion of what he wanted, and the director worked closely with the editor in the suite.

At first Hunt is mystified by Young's editing choices, chopping out of scenes early. What Terence was working towards was creating the fast tempo he and the producers felt would be essential to the film's chance of success. The editing, like the plotting, needed to be kept tight and had to moved quickly. It was a sharp learning curve for the editor, going against the then established editing practise in British film. Hunt realised they had to abandon a great deal of the received wisdom of British film making: 'The standard way of editing is you mustn't cut on movement because that creates a jump cut, but that is nonsense. I didn't wait for movement to cut from one scene to another.'

Harry Saltzman would later say a crucial ingredient for *Dr No*'s success was the fast pace. It was not shot like a British film, and it could not be edited like a British film:

'We've put into the picture a north American tempo.' The goal was to constantly drive the action forward, keeping the piece moving so fast that the audience didn't have time to question the logic. 'If you analyse *Dr No*,' said Hunt, 'there were many sequences that we didn't shoot, which we should have shot on location, and we had to make them work with inserts and lots of bits and pieces of shots back at Pinewood Studios, if you look at the film today, you'll see how the editing of it gave it a briskness and style.'

Sound editor, Norman Wanstall, who worked closely with Hunt on *Dr No*, recalled: 'Peter looked at the material we were getting and said, "I think we'd better make this move so fast, people won't have time to analyse it. Let's make it go with a bang, just before people start to analyse where it's silly or not".'

Even the approach to the audio of *Dr No* was unique. They decided that in the action scenes they would exaggerate the sound of gun shots and fists landing, creating a heightened sense of danger and excitement. This exaggerated sound was so effective in the violence sequences that, in later Bonds, they would learn it was best that, in the copy of the film sent to the censors, they omitted the enhanced audio track.

Ursula Andress, the actress that Cubby had been warned had a voice like a Dutch comic, would be dubbed by not one but two women. German voice artist Nikki Van Der Syl would provide Honey's voice as well as the voice for all the women in the film, apart from Miss Moneypenny and Miss Taro. Nikki would be a regular voice artist for the Bond films and on some of Ursula's future roles in other movies. Ursula's singing voice was supplied by British actress Diane Coupland, who also happened to be Money Norman's then wife. Hunt found he also needed to dub many of the other characters in the film, especially those filled out by amateur actors picked up in Jamaica.

The voices were not the only audio headaches. Monty Norman returned with hours of Jamaican music, some of which ended up on the soundtrack. When it came time to record the big theme tune, Young and Hunt went down to the recording studio where Monty was conducting the orchestra for the song he had been working on as a main theme. Both men were disheartened by what they heard. They just didn't think Norman's opus would work in their film.

Terence was all for junking the score and turning instead to a modern British classical composer like Sir William Walton, who had provided the soundtrack for Laurence Olivier's film version of *Hamlet*. Unfortunately for Young, the producers made it very clear that their fast-diminishing budget wasn't going to run to a big-name composer. He and his editor just had to find a way to make do with what they had. 'After all the trouble we've been through,' said Young, 'and all the problems we've overcome, if we don't have decent music in the film, it'll kill it. Then it is disaster.'

One of Hunt's assistants mentioned that he had worked on a TV programme recently which featured a jazz troupe, The John Barry Seven. Perhaps this Barry fellow might be able to help. Barry met with the director and the head of UA's music division and was asked to come up with a new arrangement of Monty's tune. 'They said, "we've got this thing, but it sounds like a funeral march,"' said Barry. '"Can you do something with it?" I never saw the movie through. I was just given a timing and told that it was this Secret Service guy. And at that time, even though I'd heard of Ian Fleming's Bond books, I'd never actually read one.'

He got paid £250 for his arrangement and was given a vague promise of work on the soundtrack of subsequent

Bond films, if there were any. Barry said: 'We recorded it at the EMI studios with lots and lots of reverb and lots of echo with the big band and it sounded very fresh.' Barry's bold, brassy version on Monty's tune will forever be instantly recognisable as the James Bond Theme. He would become synonymous with the tune and with his work on subsequent Bond soundtracks. Barry is often, erroneously, identified has the composer of the main theme. In coming years, Monty Norman would take legal action against newspapers who incorrectly identified Barry as the song's composer, and he would win. Barry's version of the Bond Theme proved enormously helpful to Peter Hunt back in the editing suite: 'We inserted the theme music every time Bond is about to do something.' It would be another signature element of the Bond franchise, reprised in every subsequent film to the expectant delight of cinemagoers. It was yet another one of those 'lucky' misfortunes that befell the production.

If Terence Young had got his way, dumped Monty's *Bad Sign, Good Sign* composition and had been given the budget to splash out on a major classical composer, there would never have been the immediately recognisable and utterly iconic Bond Theme.

Despite all the headache of pulling together the final film, Peter Hunt would become another regular in the Bond family, editing serval more of the films and directing *On Her Majesty's Secret Service*. Peter said: 'We had to do all sorts of things to make that film work, and in the end it did work. But it was a lot of hard work. *Dr No* was certainly the most difficult Bond film to edit. We eventually pulled it off with a great deal of ingenuity and a great deal of encouragement on Terence's part.' Whatever the necessities or rationale that got them there, the editor Hunt and the director Young had landed upon the cinematic equivalent of the 'Fleming Sweep'. But even at this stage, neither were aware of how special what they had created was. 'We certainly didn't think this was going to be a series,' said Hunt. 'We thought it was just a one-time thriller.' If at the time, the fast, pacy editing style seemed revolutionary it would, after the success of *Dr No*, become part of a new visual language for the screen, not just for the Bond films, but for the genre of action thrillers.

Many of the key crew members on *Dr No* would become regulars on the Bond films. Syd Cain was, like Ken Adam, an ex-RAF pilot. He was art director on the picture and contributed to Bond's style and look. When his name was accidently left off the credits, Cubby presented him with a solid gold pen as compensation, it was cheaper than redoing the prints and he would become part of the 007 franchise family. Ted Moore, the cinematographer on *Dr No*, was another crewman who would become a Bond fixture.

Maurice Binder was an American born advertising executive who had carved himself out a new career creating opening title sequences for films. He had been working in Britain from the fifties, and Cubby and Harry asked him to come up with a concept for the pre-titles sequence on their little spy film. 'That was something I did in a hurry,' said Maurice, 'because I had to get to a meeting with the producers in twenty minutes. I just happened to have little white, price tag stickers and I thought I'd use them as gun shots across the screen. We'd have James Bond walk through and fire, at which point blood comes down onscreen. That was about a twenty-minute storyboard I did, and they said, "This looks great!"' When it came to filming the sequence, he tried to use a camera sighted down the barrel of a .38 calibre pistol, but it didn't work. Instead, his team created a pinhole camera to solve the problem and, with stuntman Bob Simmons standing in for Connery, they shot the iconic opening which would become the template for the title sequence for every Bond film.

Peter Hunt said: 'Maurice always regretted not copywriting the gun barrel design, because it is used over and over and over again. He would always say to me, "dammit, why didn't I copyright it?"' Maurice would work on ever more elaborate and increasingly sexual title sequences on most of the Bond's until his death in 1991. The producers would visit the studio where he was working on filming a future Bond title sequence and find him carefully waxing down the pubic hair of one of his models, who would be dancing naked in silhouette, and wonder aloud about how they were paying him to do this work.

An American graphic artist called Joseph Caroff was given the job of designing a logo for the film. He was paid $100 for coming up with the iconic 007 signature, turning the seven into a gun, which is still used on the film's posters and merchandise today.

As the first Bond film in the franchise, *Dr No* would certainly be the toughest, most violent, and most realistic of the Bond movies of the first few decades. The humour in *Dr No*, as built up by Young and Connery, would become an essential ingredient of the franchise but, in *Dr No*, it was not as glib or silly as it would become in some of the later films. 'In a Bond film, you aren't involved in cinema-verité or avant-garde,' Terence once said. 'One is involved in colossal fun.'

In this story there was little of the gadgetry that would be on hand to assist Bond in dealing with adversaries and which would get more outlandish with each subsequent film. This tough, street version of James was a man who had to rely on his wits, his fists, and his personal strengths. Young and Connery had thought long and hard about how to take Fleming's fictional character from the pages of the books and turn him into a flesh and blood person. In their choices and decisions, they weren't just creating a more rounded, three-dimensional character for a movie. What they were doing, even if they didn't know it at the time, was setting in place the patent, the DNA, for all the Bond films to come, and not just the ones starring Connery or directed by Young. If fact, it was a formula which would go on to inspire a sizable industry of spy films and would be unashamedly stolen to improve many lesser thrillers in the decades to come.

'I knew what I wanted.' said Young, years later. 'I didn't think the picture was going to be anywhere near as popular as it was. I thought it was going to be a thing for rather highbrow tastes. I thought an awful lot of the jokes were going to be in-jokes. I think it caught on very well. When you analyse it, and this is no disrespect to Ian, the books were very sophisticated B picture movie plots. One wanted the film to have a very slick quality. We wanted to make them as sophisticated as we could, and above all, I gave the picture an enormous sense of tempo. In fact, it changed styles of filmmaking.' The head of the Cinematheque in France would agree, declaring that *Dr No* was 'one of the great innovative films. Years from now, all films will be made like this.'

But none of this was obvious to the director, his star, the crew or the producers just yet. They had taken many gambles, been forced to cut corners and settle on questionable decisions in their process of bringing James Bond to the screen. Now they just had to find out if it was going work. If it had all been worth it.

12 Are they laughing with us or at us?

A nervous Harry Saltzman and Cubby Broccoli set up a screening of a rough early print of *Dr No* for United Artists' executives, including the main man himself, Arthur Krim. When the screening ended, the lights came up and there was total silence. Saltzman remembered: 'Nobody said anything, except a man who was head of the European operation for UA. He said: "The one good thing about the picture is that we can only lose $840,000." Then they all stood up. Cubby and I were just shattered.'

Perhaps, what the executives were responding with, was simply confusion. They had made a deal with the producers and given them a million dollars to go away and make a tense, brutal thriller that was going to be heavy on violence and the sex. Certainly, *Dr No* had violence, sex and thrills but it also came with wholly unexpected humour. When the producers organised a sneak preview back in Slough, England, that was what the audience responded to, laughing throughout the film. Young, Saltzman and Broccoli had all been agreed at the pre-production stage that injecting some fun into Bond was the right way to go, but had they gone too far? Had they accidentally made a comedy spoof of a spy thriller rather than an actual spy thriller?

Johanna Harwood, the scriptwriter who had been working on the script of the film since Saltzman bought the rights, said: 'When we were working on *Dr No* everybody treated it as serious. We used to sit round having script conferences and talking about Bond's psychological approach and that kind of thing. And there was nothing comic in the books. It wasn't until the sneak preview that we had any idea we had a comedy on our hands, so to speak, because the audiences laughed.' It was Saltzman who asked the pertinent question: 'Are they laughing at Bond or laughing with him?'

At least some of the crew were unconcerned by the reaction. Lois Maxwell, who played Moneypenny, said: 'All of us who worked on the film went to a screening of the rough cut and thought it was marvellous. Instead of just being an ordinary spy film there were all these amusing bits. There was a tongue in cheek sense of humour that took the mickey out of the spy genre. That was very much Terence really.'

Wolf Mankowitz, the screenwriter who had helped bring the producers together and who had abandoned the 'piece of crap' project early, regretted his rash decision. After seeing the film, he asked the producers about getting his credit reinstated on *Dr No*, but the prints of the film had already been made.

In July 1962, Young held a private screening at the Traveller's Club in London. It was attended by Ian Fleming and his wife Ann, along with an illustrious audience that included the Duke and Duchess of Bedford and Lord and Lady Bessborough. Ann Fleming, in a letter to her friend, the writer Evelyn Waugh, said that: 'it was an abominable occasion'. Her and Ian were appalled at the laughter that greeted the scene of the tarantula crawling up Bond's body. Ann had reason to be particularly disappointed because, as she saw it, 'our fortunes depend on it'. After one screening, Fleming left the cinema with a research assistant, took a taxi directly to a pub across the road from his office, ordered a stuff drink and told his companion that it was 'dreadful, simply dreadful'.

Even the Soviet Union got in on attacking *Dr No*. They did not even wait for the film to be completed before they did. In May 1962, the Russian state newspaper *Izvestia* ran a full-page attack on *Dr No* the novel. It said the main character was a 'maniac with a screw loose', a broken-nosed beauty who likes 'to collect seashells in the nude' (Honeychile in the novel is nude and has a broken nose) and 'a great detective' by the name of James Bond. The piece asked who could be 'interested in such rubbish?'

Meanwhile the producers were having clashes with the censors in individual markets. The cold-blooded killing of Professor Dent had to be recut for some territories. While the US censors were focused on the sexual elements of the film, their UK counterparts were mostly concerned with violence. The British Board of Censors, headed by John Trevelyan, gave *Dr No* an 'A' certificate with one cut to the film, reducing the number of blows in a beating up sequence. Going forward with the franchise, Eon productions would have a long and, at times, difficult relationship with these officials, but they knew it was essential for the success of the films not to be given a restricted certificate. As Broccoli would say: 'Bond is a hard, sometimes cruel man in the films. You might even call it sadism for the family.'

Dr No was screened for the British press at the London Pavilion on 2 October 1962, before the public got to see it. The media was, to be polite, divided on its merits. *Films and Filming* magazine said: 'There hasn't been a film like *Dr No* since… when? The Mickey Spillane thrillers of the middle Fifties? *Dr No* is the headiest box-office concoction of sex and sadism ever brewed in a British studio... Just as Mike Hammer was the softening up for James Bond, so James Bond is the softening up for... what? A fascist cinema uncorrupted by moral scruples?' The reviewer then turned his fury on the censors: 'Oh, Trevelyan, art though sleeping in Soho? This is one of the X'iest films imaginable, a monstrously overblown sex fantasy of nightmarish proportions.'

The left-wing *Daily Worker* described it as 'vicious hokum skilfully designed to appeal to the filmgoers' basest feelings.' With almost all of its villains being black or Chinese, it said the film had 'sinister racist implications'. The review in *The People* was scathing: 'With Sean Connery given the job of putting him on the screen, and a million dollars spent in the process. I expected something better than this. We get a clumsy script which boobs in your face and some hammy situations that send the thrills skidding into laughs. This is NOT the way to make a good thriller.' *The Spectator* said it was 'too inept to be as pernicious as it might have been.' The review concluded by calling *Dr No* 'grotesque'.

The *Torbay Express and South Devon Echo* was more sympathetic. It was 'not an artistic masterpiece, or a film with any hidden meaning. It is intended to be entertainment. pure and simple.' A disapproving critic in the *Daily Express* complained that Bond did not behave like a traditional hero, and his methods were indistinguishable from the villains. Presumably, the journalist had not read the cartoon strip adaptations of Fleming's novels in his own newspaper, because they too detailed the cruel, sadism of this anti-hero. One reviewer, for the *Somerset Standard*, described Connery as a 'chunky Irishman' which seemed wrong on every level.

But there were also some fans among the British press. The *Liverpool Echo* said: 'Sean Connery makes James Bond a somewhat rougher diamond than had been envisioned but he handles the thick ear stuff well.' The *News of the World* stated emphatically, and prophetically: 'This new screen hero will be around for a long time.' A few years later, an article in the Vatican's newspaper would condemn *Dr No* as 'a dangerous mixture of violence, vulgarity, sadism, and sex.' Which certainly validated devout Catholic Patrick McGoohan's decision to turn down the role. However, the reprimand from the Pope likely did nothing but help the franchise at the box office.

The English poet Phillip Larkin, in his best-known work Annus Mirabilis, said sex was invented:

*'Between the end of the 'Chatterley' ban
And the Beatles' first LP.'*

The Chatterley obscenity trail ended in November 1960. The Beatles first album, *Please Please Me*, would be released in March 1963. *Dr No* premiered in London's Leicester Square on Friday 5 October 1962. Larkin had it about right. While the film may have got a mixed reception from the critics, audiences were immediately taken with this new type of British screen action hero: dangerous, violent, sexy, but also funny. Terence believed Bond arrived in the cinema at just the right moment: 'I think people were getting tired of the realistic school. The kitchen dramas and all those abortions.'

What Terence could not have seen was that a counter-culture revolution was just over the horizon, along with a British cultural invasion of the States and that Bond and Sean Connery were going to be part of it. The Beatles' debut single, *Love Me Do*, was released the same day as the film. A month or two earlier The Rolling Stones had played their first gig at the Marquee Club, just down the road in Soho. A few weeks later a satire show called *That Was The Week That Was* would premiere on the BBC, marking another signifier that this new decade was going to see a transformed Britain.

There was another striking event coinciding with the premiere of *Dr No*. Earlier in the year, Soviet leader Nikita Khrushchev and Fidel Castro, the Cuban President, reached a secret agreement to allow the Soviets to build missile sites in Cuba, and stock them with nuclear missiles. When the Americans got wind of the deal, a blockade was put on Soviet vessels travelling to Cuba, suspected of carrying missile parts. In October, the Cuban missile crisis reached its apex. Here was a very real threat to world safely, revolving around the deployment of ballistic missiles in the Caribbean region. Not for the last time would a Bond film arrive in the cinemas and its audiences find that the story on screen in some — almost prescient — way mirrors the real time dramas of the real world. A rumour had it that the head of the CIA, Allen Dulles, who was a Bond fan, had consulted Ian Fleming on the agency's next move regarding Cuba. How, he wanted to know, would Bond tackle the tricky task of dealing with Fidel Castro?

The premiere marked the moment Sean Connery became a bone fide movie star, and a new sex symbol. His amoral, violent, sexy, Bond seemed a long way away from the heroes of the year's other big films; *To Kill a Mockingbird*, *The Man Who Shot Liberty Valance* and *Lawrence of Arabia*. Too many of the traditional British leading men, including Rex Harrison, James Mason, John Mills, Trevor Howard and Laurence Olivier had a paternal way about them, more kindly than dynamic. Connery was part of this new wave of actors, alongside Burton, Finney and Harris. Men who were unashamedly not upper class; roughly hewn, capable of brutality on screen and, above all, sexual and dangerous.

Richard Maibaum, the American screenwriter who worked on the *Dr No* script and would return for future Bond films, astutely recognised what it was Connery brought to Bond. It was something that most of the other actors considered for the role could not have provided. 'The fact that Sean was a rough, tough, Scottish soccer player made him unlike the kind of English actor that Americans don't like. Sean was not the Cambridge, Whitehall type. He was a down to earth guy. The fact that we attribute to him such a high style epicure was part of the joke.'

Not long after the film's release, Connery began receiving thousands of adoring fan letters each week. When the director's friends saw Connery play Bond up on the screen, they immediately recognised the actor was impersonating Terence Young. Fleming attended the London premiere and was, publicly at least, more gracious: 'Those who've read the book are likely to be disappointed but those who haven't will find it a wonderful movie. Audiences laughed in all the right places.'

Maybe Fleming's fans might not quite see Connery as the imagined version of a blue-eyed Bond they had built up in their head from the books. However, he did embody the ruggedness and ruthlessness of their literary hero. Connery had the coldness and sadism when needed, but there was also that wry, dry humour. While he still wasn't much of a fan of the film, Fleming was warming to Sean Connery in the role: 'His height and bearing, graceful panther-like walk, the warm voice still retaining its Scots burr and his faintly rebellious air were impressive.'

In his 1964 novel, *You Only Live Twice*, Fleming filled in some of Bond's origin story, which now included a Scottish heritage and attendance at Fettes boarding school in Edinburgh, the college that had been on Connery's childhood milk delivery round. On a press junket to Italy, Connery, in hairpiece and tuxedo, and accompanied by models dressed up as glamourous 'Bond girls', was photographed 'breaking the bank' at a casino.

The newspapers breathlessly reported that Connery had successfully employed a gambling system devised by Ian Fleming to win big at the tables and the author backed up the story. It created lots of useful coverage for the film's release in Europe and was, of course, completely fake. At this point in his career, Connery was still willing to play the media game. That would change as his fame grew and the press intrusion into every aspect of his life became intolerable. He was also starting to get aggrieved at constantly being referred to as 'an overnight star'. There was some of that good old British class snobbery in the coverage of this uneducated, working class, Edinburgh milkman apparently plucked from obscurity and turned into a film star. Few members of the media seemed capable of acknowledging his years of hard work, sacrifice and dedication to his art that had made this breakthrough possible. His fear was that people would assume he was a male equivalent of Lana Turner, discovered sitting by soda fountain and turned into a star. Connery had more than paid his dues. He said: 'I have a feeling the legend is that I drove a truck into United Artists, smashed somebody on the head, dragged Cubby Broccoli up the street and said, "Make me Bond".'

Connery had now moved from the modest mews

house he shared with Diane into a much larger property that had, until recently, been home to 25 nuns from the Order of the Adoratrices. The press were enjoying the incongruity of the highly sexed, amoral James Bond let loose in a former nunnery. Diane's divorce from Anthony Shaffer, her first husband, had finally come through, and she was already pregnant with Sean's baby. A month after the premiere the couple got married in a private ceremony on Gibraltar, with two taxi drivers as witnesses. Sean knew that it would now be close to impossible for him to have a quiet wedding in London.

Connery didn't help his future relationship with the press with an interview he gave to a female journalist from the *Sunday Express*. He told the reporter that he did not think Bond was a sadist, but simply a man of passion. That would have been fine, if he had not then gone on to reveal some of his own attitudes towards women. 'I don't think there's anything wrong with hitting a woman,' he said. 'An open-handed slap is justifiable or putting your hand over her mouth. I wouldn't think I was sadistic.'

It was a quote that would get an actor cancelled immediately if he said it today. As it was, the words would be thrown back at Connery for the rest of his life, and beyond. But, back in 1962, the actor was well on his way to global celebrity and an object of lust for legions of women. If there was any threat of him becoming big headed, he only had to visit his family. When he travelled back to Edinburgh for the Scottish premiere of *Dr No*, his dad Joe greeted him: 'Hello Tam, have you been away?' If Joe was concerned about his son getting too big for his boots, he needn't have worried. As Terence Young would later say: 'With the exception of Lassie, Sean is the only person I know who's never been spoiled by success.'

Dr No was booked into the Odeon's flagship cinema

at Leicester Square, but only because of a strict picture allocation policy, which meant the owners Rank were obliged to include a quota of British made films in its schedule. Saltzman said: 'We broke every record known. They never saw such business and the most surprised were United Artists. To them, it was a B-picture. They hated it.' A nation that, post-Suez and post-Empire, was deeply unsure of itself in a radically changing world found itself with a new representative in the cinema. Connery's take on Fleming's Bond managed to be both a radical departure from the country's traditional idea of itself and yet, curiously, a reinforcement of it. *Dr No* would be one of Britain's biggest box office draws of the year. It would go on to recoup its budget just from the UK returns.

Despite the success in the home market, United Artists were still unsure of what they had on their hands with their 'Limey spy thriller'. One of their executives confidently predicted that *Dr No* 'simply would not work in America. Connery will never go over.' The film had a New York premiere on Thursday 7 March 1963, a starry event on Broadway, with Connery joined by the likes of Leonard Bernstein and Zsa Zsa Gabor on the red carpet, followed by a glamorous supper party at the Tower Suite.

The actress Shelley Winters enjoyed the *Dr No* film and went to dinner with its lead actor after a New York screening. 'He was very nervous about the film,' said Winters. 'In fact, he hated it.' Connery was already talking to her about how he could get out of his commitment to reprise the role in future films. United Artists shared his lack of faith in the movie. Saltzman and Broccoli were justifiably bewildered when *Dr No* finally opened in the US market in May. It was given a low-profile distribution, opening in 450 cinemas in the Midwest and Southwest region. When it finally reached audiences in the key markets of Los Angeles and New York, it was on a double bill with a Korean War drama, *The Young And The Brave*.

A review in the *New York World Telegram* said of Connery's performance: 'He is more than sufficiently handsome and virile. He wears his clothes elegantly. He talks with a suave mid Atlantic accent.' Other reviews were less complimentary. *Time* magazine labelled Bond 'a great big hairy marshmallow,' and 'slightly silly'. The New Republic complained that the film 'never decides whether it is suspense or suspense-spoof.' However, *Variety*, the film industry's bible, gave it an ecstatic welcome: '*Dr No* is a high-powered melodrama that crackles with intrigue and suspense and sizzles with romance. There is even some humour of a respectable level to lighten the mixture. The movie has no high-powered names, but this won't matter. *Dr No* is a perfect picture of its special kind and exactly fits that often cited but generally misunderstood category "pure entertainment".'

Another fan was Hugh Hefner, who recognised in the Bond novels something of the ethos he was cultivating in his *Playboy* magazine and burgeoning empire. Hefner's pitch for his publication was that it was created for the suave, confident, alpha male who knew how to dress well, loved the ladies and enjoyed the high life. 'Two of the major cultural phenomena to come out of the 1960s were *Playboy* and James Bond,' said Hefner, 'and they were very closely related.' Fleming had met Hefner in the late 1950s and, according to the publisher, Fleming told him over dinner: 'If James Bond was a real person, he would definitely be a *Playboy* subscriber.'

Despite UA trying to bury Bond in the drive-in theatres of the flyover states, *Dr No* was a word-of-mouth success in the America, taking in $16 million. It would make $43,500,000 globally, not bad for a $1 million investment. Cubby and Harry would remain convinced that if *Dr No* had been given the right distribution it would have made much more money for United Artists in America. Despite the studio's efforts, Eon Productions had a major hit on their hands. The triumph caught everyone by surprise. 'There was absolute panic in the production,' said Johanna. 'Because suddenly they had a huge success on their hands, and they didn't know why. And then the great panic was could they do it twice, since they didn't know why they'd done it the first time.'

Even before release of *Dr No*, Johanna had been asked to work on a draft script of *From Russia with Love*, just so they would be ready if and when UA decided on a second feature. She would again be teamed up with Maibaum and Terence Young on the script and would once again have her contribution dismissed by the men.

With *Dr No*, Eon had created a heady cocktail of thrills and sex and action and humour that the public had taken to immediately. Now they just had to go back and figure out all the ingredients in the recipe that had made it work with audiences.

There was a basic story formula. Bond is sent to investigate suspect goings on. He locates the villain and encounters his sidekicks. He infiltrates the villain's exotic lair, and, against all odds, he destroys it. There should be female relationships, of both an intimate and a deadly kind plus humour and dry comic asides. There must be an outlandish and fiendish villain along with exotic locations and impressive lairs and there also needs to be a dynamic musical soundtrack and heightened audio for the fight scenes. A provocative and increasingly sexualised title sequence is needed, and the armed and dangerous Bond must be joined by the silhouettes of beautiful, naked women. Finally, there must be that big, muscular Bond theme kicking in to inform the audiences of exactly what they were in for.

Cubby believed in big set pieces, breaking the larger film down into what were, essentially, small films in themselves. So, in *Dr No*, there was the openings episode setting up the background for the story. Then the London sequence where Bond gets his orders. The Jamaica sequence where he arrives, investigates, gets attacked, murders henchmen and beds women. Then the Crab Key sequence building to Bond's entry into Dr No's inner sanctuary leading to the explosive, destructive finale.

In a conversation with the screenwriter Richard Maibaum, Hitchcock had talked about 'bumps' in his films, referring to the memorable highpoints, shocks and thrills. He told him: 'If I have thirteen bumps, I know I have a picture.' Maibaum said: 'Broccoli, Saltzman and myself have not been content with thirteen bumps. We aim for 39. Our objective has been to make every foot of film pay off in terms of exciting entertainment.'

And of course, at the heart of the film, the charismatic, dangerous special agent. 'James Bond is very much for breaking rules,' said Connery, trying to pinpoint the character's appeal. 'He enjoys freedom that the normal person doesn't get. He likes to eat. He likes to drink. He likes his girls. He is rather cruel, sadistic.' They needed to get that formula, that unique cocktail of ingredients, exactly so and create a Bond imprint that would work in the next planned picture, *From Russia with Love*, but would also serve, if they could get everything just right, for all the Bond films that could come after that.

13 Pond water in their veins

D espite the success for *Dr No*, no one sitting in those cinemas in 1962 could have guessed they were witnessing the birth of the longest running franchise in film history. A great deal of what went right with the production of *Dr No* could be put down to 'happy accidents'. These were the result of decisions that were dictated by the limits of the slim budget, by the rigidity of the schedule and by the lost days on location. Many of their crew and cast were on board because they happened to be who was available, who they could afford, and who was willing to be part of the production. The result had been a success, a triumph. Broccoli and Saltzman had defied all the naysayers, including many at United Artists who never really believed in the film their studio was funding. They proved that James Bond could work on the big screen. That was in defiance of the many movie executives, studios and television companies and producers who, in their wisdom, had spent a decade writing off Fleming's creation as not worth bothering with.

It now didn't matter now that virtually everyone involved in *Dr No* had, at one time or another during the production, been quietly convinced that they were working on a dud that would soon be forgotten. Ursula Andress remembers the shooting of the final scene of their time at Pinewood, where she was tied to a ramp with water flooding in and Bond rescuing her in the nick of time. In some ways that scene had been emblematic of the whole production. The script had called for a tense and, typically for Fleming, sadistic torture scene. Ursula's character Honey was facing a terrible death, being slowly devoured by giant crabs.

On the day of the shoot, they discovered that the scene was no longer filmable. Their giant crabs arrived frozen their journey from Guernsey to the set and were then accidentally cooked. The production didn't have the time or the money to delay the shooting of the scene or come up with an elaborate alternative Instead, they cobbled together what they could. A very basic 'in peril' set up which would allow Bond to rescue Honey and for the story to move on. As soon as Terence Young had the scene in the can, he called 'cut'. Ursula said: 'Everyone said "okay, that's a wrap, bye bye". Nobody thought it was going to be this successful.'

Sean Connery would put it most succinctly: 'Everyone talks about how they knew the Bond films were going to be a success, but it simply isn't true.' Lightning, a really good sort of lightning, had struck *Dr No*. Now they just needed to make that lightning strike again. The core team of Connery, Young, Broccoli, Saltzman and Fleming would be present again for the next film, *From Russia with Love*. The big question was, having lucked out with a winning formula, could they avoid screwing it up second time around?

Dr No had been cobbled together from the multiple drafts of the script with four, often very conflicting writers, and then worked on again with comic asides added on the set with Connery and Young as chief collaborators. They landed on making the *Dr No* story first, because their first choice was involved in litigation, and they figured *Dr No* would be the cheapest to make. Location delays led to missing scenes and unexplained jumps in the narrative. These in turn helped convince the director and editor that they needed to create a fast, choppy, editing style that defied all traditional editing techniques just to cover the cracks.

Key roles were filled by people who were not their first, or even second or third choice. Often it was because they were the last man standing, or, in the case of Bernard Lee, whoever happened to be available on that day. Many of the smaller parts were filled by amateurs they happened across on location. And, somehow, all those small 'happy accidents' had fallen into place. All the team needed to do now was to figure out what elements had made *Dr No* work, and then repeat and enhance them.

Editor Peter Hunt said: 'Terence Young was very nervous. Doing the second one was not easy. After you had a success with the first one, you go into the second one and just hope to God it's going to be all right. But as it happened, it wasn't just all right, it got better. Everything in it was better. After that, everyone was much more confident. Attitudes were better, and people were looking forward to the challenge. Budgets were suddenly bigger, and one was able to try more adventurous stuff. And it also allowed us to take a little bit more time, perhaps, and a bit more money allowed for us to indulge and experiment.' They tried to assemble as many of the same team that made *Dr No* as they could. That included the scripting duo of Maibaum and Harwood, with Young adding his thoughts and input. The novelist Berkely Mather was also brought back in and consulted on the script.

After John Barry produced his memorable arrangement of the Bond Theme, the producers had promised him work on future Bond films. They were as good as their word, and he came on board to take care of the soundtrack for *From Russia with Love*. Barry would become synonymous with the Bond franchise. The producers had temporarily fallen out with Maurice Binder and a New York graphic designer, Robert Brownjohn, was brought in for the opening sequence of *From Russia with Love*. His key innovation was to project screen images across the bodies of beautiful models and film the results. Binder would re-join the Eon firm on later films.

Bernard Lee returned as the disapproving fatherly 'M'. Eunice Gayson would make her second and final appearance as Bond's girlfriend Sylvia Trench and Lois Maxwell was back as Miss Moneypenny, all providing a level of continuity with the first film. For Eunice, officially the first on screen Bond girl back in that casino scene in *Dr No*, the Bond films had been a liberation for women in the industry. 'Before then we were always the little wife part or the sister or the aunt or whatever,' said Eunice. 'We weren't allowed to be sexy. Cleavage, what's that? Things changed because the film world discovered British women were sexy. They had never been allowed to see them in that role. I think the revolution for English actresses in films occurred with *Dr No*. It changed the face of filming in Britain and probably throughout the world.'

Major Boothroyd had now become the Quartermaster for MI6 and would become known as 'Q', with Desmond Llewelyn joining the cast. He would become another regular, introducing as he did the wonderful world of the spy accessories. In *From Russia with Love*, Q hands over a new piece of kit to Bond, a uniquely adapted briefcase. The case, created by Syd Cain, would be the commencement of Bond's long association with fantastic gadgetry. It came complete with a 22. Calibre rifle, 50 gold sovereigns, spring loaded knife and a tear gas cartridge set to discharge when it was opened incorrectly. The scene with Q also set up another standard sequence for the coming films, with an irritated Q admonishing Bond for his general lack of respect and care for the expensive toys he is given to play with.

Peter Hunt was back on board as editor. He would edit five films in the series and take the director seat in the sixth. Hunt felt he now had a good handle on the appeal and the audience for Bond. 'What Ian Fleming wrote were paperbacks for all the suburban people who spent every day travelling backwards and forwards to work on a train and needed something for a thrill.' Why, figured Hunt, could we not make paperback films?

United Artists, once they realised that a sexy, explosive thriller which also made audience laugh could be big box office, were eager for delivery of the next film. The budget was double what it had been for *Dr No*. Ken Adam, the man who had done such an exemplary job as set designer, had to remove himself from the second picture. Ironically, his work on *Dr No* was the reason he was not available. '[Stanley] Kubrick, after seeing *Dr No*, contacted me and asked if I would like to meet him,' said Adam. 'I met this boyish youngish man, we were all pretty young in those days, he liked the look of *Dr No* and asked me to design *Dr Strangelove*.' Adam would win a Bafta award for his work on Kubrick's film and would return to the Bond fold to make his mark on later films.

Syd Cain took up Adam's role in *From Russia with Love*. By contrast with Adam's meagre budget on *Dr No*, Cain got to spend $150,000 creating just one single set, for the chess game in the film.

The Bond girl department was led by a young Italian actress Daniela Bianchi who played Tatiana Romanova, a cypher clerk who lures Bond to Istanbul as part of an intricate double cross. There were more of the ad libs and the double entendres. When Tatiana apologises for her small mouth, Bond assured her: 'It's the right size, for me, that is.' A more attentive censor might not have been happy to let that line pass.

The film introduced two new memorable villains. Robert Shaw playing Donald 'Red' Grant, an assassin hired by SPECTRE and placed on Bond's trail to avenge for the murder of Dr Julius No. And there was a new twist on the Bond woman. Lotte Lenya played the sinister and deadly SPECTRE Number Three, Rosa Klebb. Her name was a play on the Soviet propaganda slogan for women's rights, 'Bread and Roses'. Lenya had been married to the composer Kurt Weill and was part of the playwright Bertolt Brecht's pre-war ensemble in Berlin. She was the original Jenny in their masterpiece, *The Threepenny Opera*.

Bob Simmons was unavailable to be the main stunt coordinator, but he did do some stunt work for the film. Harry Saltzman was eager that Bond should show his violent side in this second outing. He got his wish with the brutal and powerful fight scene on the Orient Express between Bond and his would-be assassin Grant. Fleming had been inspired by the real-life case in the 1950s of an American naval attaché who was assassinated on the Orient Express by a Soviet agent. In preparation for their big fight, both actors were tutored in Greek wrestling. The scene lasts a few minutes in the film but took three weeks to shoot. Istanbul, along with stopovers in Venice and Paris, provided the exotic backdrops this time. Anthony Dawson, last seen lying prone on a Jamaican bedroom floor as the slain Professor Dent, makes an uncredited reappearance as Blofeld, the head of SPECTRE.

The producers now had $2 million to play with, although the production still managed to go over budget and over schedule. It also had its share of on-set mishaps, and potential tragedies. Connery came close to serious injury after a helicopter, flown by an inexperienced pilot and filming one of his scenes at sea, came too close to the boat he was in and nearly clipped him. Young and a photographer almost drowned when their helicopter crashed into the sea while filming a key sequence of the film and they had to be rescued. Terence, arm in a sling, was back in his director's chair and working 30 minutes later. Daniela Bianchi had been involved in a car accident on the way to the set which had left her with bruises on her face, which led to delays in the schedule. The Mexican character actor, Pedro Armendáriz, who had been cast to play Bond's friend and associate, Kerim Bey, was diagnosed with terminal cancer. He insisted on completing the shoot, wanting to leave money to his family. He was too ill for some of his scenes, and Terence had to stand in for him. Armendariz would die at his own hand in hospital, four months before the film's release.

Kerim's murder in the film is a personal blow to Bond. He was the 'sacrificial lamb' for this screen outing. As the poster for *From Russia with Love* promised: 'Meet James Bond... his new incredible women... his new incredible enemies... his new incredible adventures...

When From Russia with Love was released in 1963, it would be an even greater success at the world's box offices than its predecessor. The die was cast. In a sign of their new confidence, it was the first of the movies to sign off with the promise: 'Bond will return...' signposting the next Bond film. The team had taken on the lessons of what had worked from the first outing, and they improved on the recipe. They cultivated and built up the humour, and created a tight, fast tempo film with the requisite beautiful women, the violence, the villains, the thrills and the exotic locations. Young was not alone when he ranked *From Russia with Love* as the best of the Bond pictures. 'Not because I directed it, although I think it's well directed, but because it was the best subject for a Bond film.' Broccoli placed it in his top three Bonds: 'It was with this film that the Bond style and formula were perfected.' Connery also contended that it was his favourite: 'The first one I think was shot very well in the circumstances we had. In terms of the time we had and the budget. I think Terence Young did it marvellously. The second one I think is the best of them all, That's my opinion.'

A few years earlier John F Kennedy had provided a very welcome boost to the profile of Fleming's hero in the States, by claiming *From Russia with Love* as one of his favourite books. In November 1963, the President attended a special screening of the film of his favourite Fleming novel in the White House, just before he headed off on a campaign stop to Dallas.

One key indicator of Bond's impact would be the avalanche of movies that sought, in one way or another, to cash in on the spy thriller phenomena. *The Man From UNCLE* was a television series about a pair of spies, one American and one Russian, who work together during the height of the Cold War. Ian Fleming had been an early consultant on the series, which started airing in 1964. It was Fleming who, apparently, came up with the name Napoleon Solo for the lead character. The series would run for several years and spawn several film versions as well as a short-lived spin off, *The Girl from UNCLE*.

Mission Impossible was another multimedia franchise that launched in the mid-sixties. It featured a team of secret agents who took on all the jobs that just seemed too complex to solve. Tom Cruise is still making *Mission Impossible* films today. In another sixties television series *I*

Spy, Bill Cosby and Robert Culp played a couple of tennis bums travelling the world playing tournament matches as a guise for their undercover work dealing with spies and villains.

Patrick McGoohan's *Dangerman* had been cancelled but following the success of the Bond flicks, it got a revamp for the US market. Its theme tune, Secret Agent Man, became a chart hit. The crimefighters of *The Avengers* had started on British television in 1961, but it would not be until 1965 that it became one of the few British-produced shows to make it to prime time on American television. Bond had certainly helped make the US a welcome territory for 'limey' secret agents.

In 1966 a cartoon strip character, *Modesty Blaize*, got transferred on to the big screen. An independent minded swinging sixties woman, played by Italian actress Monica Vitti, helped the British secret service foil a daring jewellery raid. Even the Soviets, who had gone out of their way to attack Fleming's hero and the Bond films, got in on the act. A Soviet super-spy Colonel Maxim Maximovich Isayev, codenamed Stierlitz, would appear in a series of novels which, like their British counterpart, get translated onto the screen. Stierlitz was very much made with the approval of the KGB. He was a more righteous and less decadent agent than Bond with no time for woman. Although he did have a taste for vodka and singing patriotic Russian folk songs.

In 1968, Russian television broadcast a four-part spy series *The Shield and the Sword*. The series, based on novels written by the Secretary of the Soviet Writers Union, followed the wartime exploits of a fictional Russian spy who travels into Nazi Germany and infiltrate German military intelligence. This story of a cool, fearless secret agent taking on the enemies of the Soviet Union proved hugely popular. It also inspired a teenage Vladimir Putin to think about a career in the KGB. Apparently, what impressed the young Putin was that here was one man who could achieve what an entire army could not.

Somewhat surprisingly, Cubby was still sharing his office with Irving Allen, his former partner and the man who had scuppered his chances of obtaining the rights to Fleming's novel back in the 1950s. It would be disconcerting for members of the Bond production team, coming in to discuss work on whatever was the upcoming Bond film, to have Irving earwigging on their conversation from the other side of the room.

Despite his previous assertion then that the secret agent had not been good enough for TV, Irving also got on the movie spy business. He produced a stream of films about a character named Matt Helm, a louche, fun loving playboy photographer who works for an American counter espionage agency in his spare time. Dean Martin played the title role.

Art director Peter Lamont remembered discussing a possible gimmick for one of the Bond movies with Cubby in the office. It was never used by Eon, he said, but somehow it did turn up in a later Matt Helm movie. One utterly shameless rip off was *O.K. Connery*, a 1967 Italian comedy thriller starring Neil Connery, Sean's younger brother, playing James Bond's younger brother. It managed to recruit into its supporting cast Bond regulars Lois Maxwell and Bernard Lee as well as Anthony Dawson from the first two Bond films. Sean was not best pleased with Lois and Bernard agreeing to appear in the spoof, when he met them back on the set of the next Bond film.

The first comedy spoof after the release of *Dr No*, was *Carry On Spying* featuring a villain named 'Dr Crow, and a criminal organisation called STENCH (the Society for the Total Extinction of Non-Conforming Humans). The only man standing in their way to world domination is secret agent 'Charlie Bind', played by Charles Hawtrey, and aided by 'Daphne Honeybutt', played by Barbara Windsor. Its producers had intended to call Hawtrey's character 'James Bind - 001 and a half' but changed it after an irate Saltzman and Broccoli threatened to sue. Inevitably, a spoof spy television series came along with the bumbling secret agent Maxwell Smart in *Get Smart*, created by Mel Brooks.

In the cinemas, James Coburn played Derek Flint, a superspy with the Z.O.W.I.E. (Zonal Organization World Intelligence Espionage) agency who is brought out of retirement to tackle a group of mad scientists who want to control the weather. In the follow up film, *In Like Flint*, Derek had to foil an international feminist conspiracy to topple the US government and replace it with a feminist matriarchy. The Bond franchise would continue to influence the output of rival filmmakers for decades to come, from the Bourne movies to Austin Powers and his adventures.

In early 2020, there was one story, and only one story, dominating the global news agenda: Covid. On every news bulletin in every country, on every continent, it was the same. Daily press conferences with politicians, doctors, and scientists. Updates on death tolls. Overwhelmed hospital. New and increasingly strict safety measures. Scarcity of masks. Lockdown restrictions. Deserted streets. Empty office blocks. Factories and businesses shut down. Airports and transport systems closed. Entire cities and countries on strict curfew.

A rare item of showbusiness trivia muscled its way to the top of the global headlines. The release of the 25th Bond film, starring Daniel Craig, had been postponed indefinitely. Just why would the non-opening of an action movie be a major story during a pandemic? Over the past sixty years James Bond has become a unique global brand. And, like it or not, the release of a new Bond film has become a major cultural event. The films have, in a unique way, become a barometer for Britain and for the world. They act as a mirror to an ever-shifting society and a precursor of changes coming upon us.

In October 1962, as *Dr No* was getting its premiere in London, the Cuban Missile Crisis was breaking out. It gave this modest, low-budget British thriller more of an edge and a certain prescience. It was as if Fleming and the film makers had a secret insight into global politics. Throughout the life of the Bond cycle, there would be times when the movies seemed to reflect back to its audiences the real-time global events going on around them as well as their concerns about the fate of the world. From solar energy and climate change to Space Wars. From the growth of Silicon Valley to Cyber Terrorism.

And when audience members finally got to see *No Time To Die*, some of the more conspiracy minded who find the storyline, about a lab created biological weapon that threatens much of the world population, had an uncomfortable connection with what they were living through. This latest film had another resonance for many people in the global film business. The release of *No Time To Die* and its success or failure was nothing less than a bellwether for the entire industry.

As the actors playing Bond changed, their different take on the role seemed to reflect the age, from the camp 1970s of Roger Moore, to Timothy Dalton's 'Bond on the edge of a nervous breakdown' in the eighties, and onwards. *Dr No* made a belated entry into the #MeToo conversation when Marguerite LeWars, the former Miss Jamaica recruited to play Julius No's photographer Annabel Chung, broke a sixty-year silence on the behaviour of her director. Marguerite had been sharing a limousine with Terence Young as they travelled to a wrap party at the end of shoot. In 2022, Marguerite told a Bond fan podcast: 'Sorry to say but Terence became aggressive, making a pass. He grabbed at me, I slapped him across the face. He grabbed me again and I slapped him again. And I said I will hurt you if you touch me again.' Young then threatened to cut her out of the film. 'I said go ahead Mr Young, I have already been paid.' When, a few months later, he called to ask her to fly to London for overdubbing, she refused.

In the modern era, Bond has become dangerously close to being 'woke'. In this most recent incarnation, Bond is presumed dead and another agent, played by a black actress, Lashana Lynch, temporarily takes on the mantle of 007. Around the time of its eventual release, that film's director Cary Fukunaga called out the earlier incarnation of screen Bond as a rapist. 'Is it *Thunderball* or *Goldfinger* where basically Sean Connery's character rapes a woman?' said Fukunaga. 'She's like 'No, no, no,' and he's like, 'Yes, yes, yes.' That wouldn't fly today.' It is unlikely that Ian Fleming would have been happy with the appraisal. But then maybe that's not the point. Perhaps he also wouldn't have cared for 'M' being played by a woman or for 'Q' to come out as gay. For sixty years, Bond has been mirroring the world and its shifting morals, values and concerns and projecting them back to it. Here was a sexist alpha male character that, by many people's estimations, should have been, in the 21st century, dismissed as a fossil, a dinosaur. The Bond production machine has avoided that fate by responding to the changing world by constantly adapting itself.

In the 1950s, Fleming had been disturbed to discover

that his novels were being avidly read by schoolboys. He wrote them, he said, for an adult audience and he certainly didn't want James Bond to be a role models for future generations. How then would he have felt when the organisers of the 2012 London Olympics managed to persuade Her Majesty The Queen to play herself in Games' opening, alongside Daniel Craig's Bond? Bond is now the most globally recognised 20th Century Briton, after The Queen and Winston Churchill.

Back in the sixties, Saltzman spelled out in plain English the core message audiences should take from the Bond films: 'We have no message to sell. We want to entertain people. That's the only barometer we have.' It is not a point that seemed to have got through to the politicians, who understood there was something more powerful going on with this screen character. John F Kennedy apparently said he wished that he had a James Bond to help him out during the Cuba Missile Crisis, He would not be the last US President to see in Bond a potent symbol of the West and Western democracy and values. 'As I see it 007 is really a modern-day version of the great heroes who have appeared from time to time in our great history,' said Ronald Reagan. 'There were many like him in the past, pioneers, soldiers, lawmen, explorers, people who all went out and put their lives on the line for the cause of good. Bond is fearless, skilled, witty, courageous, optimistic and one other thing, he always gets his girl. James Bond is a man of honour. Maybe it sounds old fashioned, but I think he is a symbol of real value to the free world.'

Bill Clinton, another former resident of the Oval Office, said: 'You get why presidents like Bond. The good guys win. It's immensely reassuring to people.' Donald Trump will go down in history for many reasons. However one minor one will be as the first U.S. president since Dwight

Eisenhower to not have a James Bond movie released during his tenure.

CIA boss Allen Dulles reportedly told Fleming the agency had tried out some of Bond's trickery in real life, but without success. Perhaps Dulles recognised that what was more important in Bond, more than the madcap schemes and outlandish plots, was what he represented. In the globally successful Bond films, the West had a popular and powerful entertainment figure that cast Western intelligence services in a favourable light.

It was an observation that was not lost of the Soviets. The Russian newspaper *Izvestia* labelled Fleming as a tool of great imperialist enemy. 'American propagandists must be in a bad way if they need recourse to the help of an English freebooter — a retired spy turned mediocre writer.' Fleming and his publishers had considered using the quote on the back of his next Bond paperback but, in the end, decided against it.

Bond films could not be publicly screened in the Soviet Union. However they were compulsory viewing for all KGB agents, who at least recognised compelling propaganda for Western ideals when they saw it. One of those young agents would have been Vladimir Putin, who joined the KGB in 1975, around the time of the release of *The Man with the Golden Gun.*

The phrases 'plotline of a Bond movie' or 'Bond villain' are often bandied around whenever a journalist, or a politician, seeks to convey a simple narrative about a complex global conflict, or crisis, or an opponent.

As the current President of Russia, Putin has repeatedly and credibly been accused of sending his ruthless operatives to carry out murders in the name of the State. A secret agent with a licence to kill does not seem so glamourous and heroic when thugs from a foreign power carelessly spread a cruel and deadly nerve agent around a cathedral town in the heart of England. Their aim was to kill a retired, and now harmless, former Soviet official. They ended up poisoning ordinary civilians and murdering an innocent woman.

If the Soviets attacked the central principles and mores of the Bond stories, they were not alone. John Le Carre was another British writer of Cold War spy novels that were successfully brought to the screen. The creator of George Smiley was irritated that his output was constantly compared with Fleming's. 'I think it's a great mistake if one is talking about espionage literature to include Bond in this genre at all,' he said. 'It seems to me he is more of an international gangster with as said, a licence to kill. He is a man with unlimited movement, but a man without any political context. It is of no interest to Bond who is, for instance, President of the United States, or who is President of the Union of Soviet Republics. It's the consumer goods ethic really, that everything around you, all the dull things of life, are suddenly animated by this wonderful cache of espionage. The things on our desks that could explode, our ties which could suddenly take photographs. These tie to a drab and materialistic existence a kind of magic that does not really exist.'

The influential British journalist and commentator Christopher Hitchens was another critical voice: 'Not for Fleming the moral ambiguities and shady compromises of a Graham Greene or John le Carre. Every line that he composed was either overt or subliminal propaganda for the great contest with Communism, and all of the subordinate themes, from racism to sadism, were ancillary to it.'

Ian Fleming would likely have brushed away all this criticism aimed at what was intended as a fantasy hero written as popular entertainment for an adult audience. 'Bond is not a hero,' he said, 'nor is he depicted as being very likable or admirable. He is a Secret Service agent. He's not a bad man, but he is ruthless and self-indulgent. He enjoys the fight. He also enjoys the prizes. In fiction people used to have blood in their veins. Nowadays they have pond water. My books are just out of step. But then so are all the people who read them.'

After the release of *Dr No*, the influential French New Wave critic turned director François Truffaut sounded a warning for all film makers. He believed the film 'marked the beginning of the period of decadence in the cinema. For the first time throughout the world, mass audiences were exposed to a type of cinema that relates neither to life nor to any romantic tradition but only to other films and always by sending them up.' If he was worried about the influence the film would have on future audiences and the future of cinema, then he would be dismayed at just how successful the franchise has become. At least half the earth's population has seen a Bond movie.

Sean Connery and Ursula Andress in *Dr No*.

14 Gamblers, before they die, are often given a great golden streak of luck

*F*rom *Russia with Love* would mark the last collaboration of the unique group of men that did so much to create the Bond universe on film. By the time the third screen instalment, *Goldfinger*, premiered in September 1964, Ian Fleming was dead. The heavy drinking and chain-smoking had finally caught up with him. Right up until the end, Fleming ignored the doctors' warnings that he needed to radically change his lifestyle. On such matters, Ian Fleming was in total agreement with James Bond when, in the novel, *You Only Live Twice*, his character said:' I shall not waste my days in trying to prolong them, I shall use my time.'

Despite being aware of Fleming's opposition to him taking the role, Connery had developed a kind of friendly rapport with the writer. He was, Connery remembered: 'A terrific snob, but very good company, tremendous knowledge, spoke German and French, got an interview with Stalin one time when he was working for Reuters.'

In 1960 Fleming made an entry in his notebook on the death of the famed socialite, horse trainer and diplomat Aly Khan: 'Gamblers just before they die are often given a great golden streak of luck. They get gay and young and rich and then, when they have been sufficiently flattered by the fates, they are struck down.' By the time Ian Fleming succumbed to heart disease in August of 1964, at the age of 56, he had sold 10 million copies of the Bond novels in the US alone. He had also lived to see his long-cherished dream of watching Bond up on the big screen realised.

But what had been achieved with his fictional hero would be more than that. By 1964 Bond was on his way to becoming a screen icon, a character who was a film star in his own right. One who would continue to be a draw for world audiences for decades, irrespective of whoever took on the role. By the time Fleming handed in the manuscript of *The Man with the Golden Gun* to his editor, William Plomer, he knew it would be the last one he produced. He apologised to Plomer for the state of his final book and confessed that he had run out of 'both puff and zest'.

Since his death, a small army of writers have kept new Bond books flowing into the shops, with varying degrees of satisfaction from the fans. Terence Young, after directing the first two Bonds and putting his indelible stamp on them, declined to return for *Goldfinger*. After his success with *Dr No* and *From Russia With Love*, he was deluged with offers. He chose to make *The Amorous Adventures of Moll Flanders* next. There had been some discussion of the husband-and-wife team of Connery and Diane Cilento taking the leads in this raunchy period comedy romance. In the end, the parts went to Kim Novak and Richard Johnson. The film would suffer from the fifty-nine cuts forced on them in the US 'in the interests of American morality,' said the director dryly. Terence obviously hadn't made the sex funny enough to slip by the censors.

For *Goldfinger*, the producers turned to Guy Hamilton, one of their original choices for the director seat. Young would come back to direct one more Bond film with

Thunderball. He continued making films for another twenty years, although nothing that matched the success of Bond. In 1966, he directed *Triple Cross*, a loose adaptation of the life of Eddie Chapman, the safecracker turned double agent that Terence had befriended thirty years earlier. The film flopped, despite a cast that included Christopher Plummer, Trevor Howard and Romy Schneider. The public, it seemed, preferred the made-up antics of the 007 secret agent to the real thing.

One of Terence's most effective post Bond films was *Wait Until Dark*, a thriller about a blind woman menaced by gangsters who believe there are drugs hidden in her apartment. It would be the only film Terence made with Audrey Hepburn who, as a volunteer nurse, had taken care of him when he was wounded and recuperating in a Dutch hospital during the war. Hepburn was nominated for an Oscar for her performance and the film is regarded now as one of the best thrillers of the decade. Young had turned down the producers' offer of a percentage deal on the profits of the Bond films he directed, preferring to be paid a higher wage up front. He had that lavish lifestyle to support. It was not a wise long-term financial decision. Not that he ever seemed to complain about it.

Young claimed the producers had asked him back to direct Bond two more times and both times he declined. It would be up to other directors to further refine and define the Bond character. 'Terence Young was a phenomenal character,' said special effects supervisor John Stears, who'd work with him on all three of his Bond films. 'He would just absolutely get into your mind what he was thinking. You'd do things for Terence without thinking. You'd just do it because you knew that was what had to be done.'

'The style that is associated with James Bond comes from Terence's style,' said Michael G Wilson, Cubby Broccoli's stepson who would take up the mantel of co-producer on later Bond films. 'The clothes and restaurants and the food and the wine and all of those kind of things are Terence Young. He brought that flair.' Young might have been the main man responsible for injecting humour into the role of Bond, but he had been a strict disciplinarian. He maintained a careful balance between the seriousness of the story and the funny asides. It would be many films into the Bond franchise before the public would see a Bond quite as violent as in his 007 films.

Later, less disciplined directors would let the humour and the quips become almost overpowering and the films descend into something very close to farce. Like the increasing overreliance on the gadgetry and special effects, the humour would at times overshadow both the character of Bond and the urgency of his mission.

Terence died at the age of 79 in Cannes, France in 1994. He was still in the business of making films, working on a documentary at the time. Ken Adam said there had been a special bond formed between the director and his leading man. 'He adored Sean and Sean adored Terence. Terence had, certainly as far as I am concerned, no ego problem. He had enormous panache; he was never worried about inviting the whole crew to a party of caviar and champagne.'

Connery was of course back as Bond, fulfilling his contractual obligations, but there was in him a growing unhappiness at playing the role, He would soon begin to refer to Bond as 'Frankenstein's monster' as well as complaining about working for a pair of producers who, he felt, undervalued his contribution.

Dr No had been a box office success. With *From Russia with Love*, they had a major hit on their hands and the franchise, (not a word much used about films in the sixties) had been established. Then in 1964, with the massive success of *Goldfinger*, they found they now had a cultural phenomenon. By the middle of the decade Connery was the number one box office draw in the world. Woman were throwing themselves at him and he was not exactly pushing them away.

With each film Sean demanded, and received, more money, rightly believing that he had played a major role in the box office successes. Cubby had a point when he said, back when they were hunting for their lead actor on *Dr No*, that Bond would be the real star of the movie and whoever played Bond would become a star. He was right, up to a point. It is difficult to imagine David Niven or Rex Harrison would have brought the dangerous, magnetic energy and sense of danger to the role that Connery imparted. Or that they would have turned Bond into a cultural phenomenon to match that other British, sixties' craziness, Beatlemania.

The comparisons with The Beatles were not hyperbolic. Like the Fab Four, Connery was now constantly at the centre of press and public hysteria. Years later, he would say: 'I had no awareness of that scale of reverence and pressure and what have you. It was around the same time as The Beatles. The difference was they had four of them to kick around and to blame each other. I made as many mistakes as anybody in dealing with it. I found it a bit of a nightmare to deal with actually.'

Sean would try the patience of the duo of producers, but they had him under contract, and they were desperate not to lose their leading man anytime soon. 'The difference with this guy,' said Broccoli, trying to sum up Connery's appeal, 'is the difference between a still photograph and film. When he starts to move, he comes alive.' When asked about rumours of their strained relationship, Saltzman managed to be diplomatic about their demanding lead actor: 'No star is easy but he's alright. We have our differences, but the pictures get made.'

This star was understandably fearful of being typecast in the one role and eager to take on other, more challenging, and radically different parts. He was already starting to get his pick of offers to work with directors of the calibre of Alfred Hitchcock and Sidney Lumet. Hitchcock was at the height of his powers in the early 1960s after the success of *The Birds* and *Psycho*. When he approached Connery to play the lead male role in *Marnie*, the actor asked to see the script. Connery was concerned that he might end up in a movie like Hitchcock's *North by Northwest*, which had been a key inspiration for the style and humour of *Dr No*. Hitchcock tartly replied that Cary Grant, who had made four films with the director, never asked to see a script.

'I'm not Cary Grant,' retorted Connery.

He also starred in *The Hill*, a stark British black and white drama set in a military prison, made by the American director Sidney Lumet. The film failed at the box office, but it was a deeply satisfying project for Connery. It showed he could take on tough, challenging roles that were miles away from the debonair spy. It would be the first of five films he would make with Lumet. Connery had spent much of the fifties struggling to convince directors and producers that he was worth casting in roles that were more challenging than a bouncer or a truck driver or a one-line bit player. Now he had a new, and even more daunting, mountain to climb. To convince audiences around the world that they should pay good money to see him in roles other than a suave, well dressed secret agent.

'I'd been an actor since I was 25,' said Connery, 'but the image that the press put out was that I just fell into this tuxedo and started mixing vodka martinis, and of course, it was nothing like that at all. I'd done television, theatre, a

231

whole slew of things. But it was more dramatic to present me as someone who had just stepped in off the street.'

His mate, and fellow actor Michael Caine, said: 'If you were his friend in these early days you didn't raise the subject of Bond. He was, and is, a much better actor than just playing James Bond, but he became synonymous with Bond. He'd be walking down the street and people would say, "Look, there's James Bond". That was particularly upsetting to him.'

The problem was these damned spy films overshadowed everything else. On top of that, the punishing and increasing lengthy shooting schedules required to make them meant it was difficult for Connery to commit to other films. Sean now had something more that connected him to Ian Fleming. Bond had been enormously beneficial to both, changing their lives and bringing wealth and fame. But then, like Fleming, Connery felt trapped by the secret agent, pressured to keep churning out Bond stories in an unrelenting circle of success. 'I'd like to kill him,' he once said of his alter ego.

As the budgets increased — *Goldfinger*'s was set at $3 million, the same as the first two films combined — the shoots got longer, the locations more exotic, the set pieces more ambitious and, inevitably, the schedules overran. That made it extremely difficult for the lead actor to commit to any of the other projects he was desperate to do.

While filming a fight scene with Japanese wrestler turned actor Harold Sakata, who played the henchman Oddjob in *Goldfinger*, Connery suffered a painful back injury. It didn't help that the actor was already in yet another money dispute with the producers, In the end everything was settled, and Cubby and Harry agreeing to pay him 5 per cent of the box office gross of any future Bond films he starred in. Each film needed to be more successful than the last. The pressure was to make the next Bond bolder, bigger, and more ambitious. The production team were driven by the fear that, if the new one didn't top the spectacle of the previous film, audiences would go home disappointed.

That meant the budgets got fatter. The explosions got louder. The villains' lairs more expansive. The stunts more daring. The gadgetry became wilder and madder. The special effects team were constantly being asked to come up with new thrills the audience hadn't seen before. Sean grew disillusioned by all this technology and high-tech equipment that now came as standard in each Bond film: 'It was always important for me to use the humanity of the character as a base because however original the gadgets were, James Bond still had to figure his way out. It's the human being, with all his human instincts, who must overcome the obstacles. But they kind of lost that in the plots.'

By the time they got to Connery's fifth outing, *You Only Live Twice*, his relationship with the producers was such that he refused to act if either of them was on the set. His relationship with the acerbic Saltzman was particularly bad. Connery understood how important Bond had been in turning him into a leading man. It had opened doors and allowed him opportunities that he was unlikely to have ever been considered for without the role. He also knew that the producers had taken a major gamble on him, having to convince United Artists, Fleming, and everyone else, to allow him to play Bond. But how many films did he owe them before he could say he had repaid that faith in him?

During the filming of *You Only Live Twice*, the international press descended on Japan where most of the location shooting was taking place. The media frenzy around Connery was such that the production team had to hire 30 extra security guards just to keep people off the set. Local photographers were trying to grab snaps of Connery in the toilet. It was a deeply unhappy experience and half-way through filming Connery announced this was his last Bond film. The producers, exhausted, and not wanting to disrupt filming on *You Only Live Twice*, agreed. Connery would be persuaded to return for a final Bond outing with Eon, after George Lazenby had taken over the role in just one film, *On Her Majesty's Secret Service*.

For *Diamonds Are Forever*, Sean would be tempted back with an offer of $1.4 m plus a percentage of the box office — a bit of a step up from the £6,000 he was paid for *Dr No*. 'It was an unprecedented deal in those days,' said Tom Mankiewicz, who co-wrote the Diamonds script. Connery donated his salary to the Scottish International Education Trust, which helped underprivileged Scottish children. For Sean, the issue of recompense was less to do with the actual money and more about ensuring he was getting respect and getting paid his due.

'I have discovered a latent hatred for injustice,' said Connery in an interview in the late 1960s. 'And I feel that it's being going on for such a long time, particular with producers. There is a lot of freeloading that goes on. A period of making a film can take up to seven, eight months. In all that time, they can have all their accommodation paid, cars, bills picked up, and they do live like gangsters. If there is a producer, be they male or female or a bit of both, in this world who will give a fair deal to any actor or actress, he will get any actor and actress who will work for them for any amount, if they are fair.'

There had been some jitters on the Las Vegas location shoot of Diamonds when, one day, Harry Saltzman turned up on set unexpectantly. The entire crew were aware of Connery's fractious relationship with the producer and wondered how the star would react. In the end, Sean went straight up to Harry, grabbed him by the shoulders and gave him a big kiss on the forehead. The producer turned red and retreated. He flew back from the shoot the next day, never to return. At the end of the filming, Connery announced to the crew that he would 'never again' don the 007 mantel. Appropriately enough, the scene he shot last during the schedule for Diamonds was where an unconscious James Bond is placed in a coffin in a funeral parlour.

But still the producers were not yet ready to give up. They asked Mankiewicz, who was now working on the script for the next Bond, *Live and Let Die*, to see if he could persuade Sean to return to the role, just one last time. Mankiewicz met up with the actor for lunch: 'I worked up the courage and said, "You know Sean, this next Bond is going to be so much fun," and he said to me, "And I have an obligation to my public to play James Bond? Well, when does that obligation stop? Seven films? Ten films? Twenty films? I've been playing this part for a decade or more. When do I no longer have an obligation to the public to play James Bond?"'

Saltzman, for one, liked to insist that the role was bigger than the guy who played him: 'Somewhere in a rep company in a place like the Midlands, we're going to come across an actor who will fit the role perfectly.' They didn't have to hunt that hard. Roger Moore, briefly considered in the original search, would make his debut as Bond in *Live and Let Die*.

Connery's relationship with Cubby was certainly better than with Harry, although he was capable of flinging mud liberally at either producer: 'They're both sitting on £50 million and looking across the desk at each other and thinking: "that bugger's got half of what should be mine".'

Cubby, the personable one, the one who was everyone's friend on set, was hurt by Sean's jibes: 'I was the only one he could deal with. He really hated Saltzman. I never had a problem with him until after he left our domain and he started saying terrible things about me.' Cubby would be even more hurt when the actor attempted to sue Broccoli and MGM-UA Entertainment claiming he was still owed money, based on profits from the early films of the franchise. The eventual settlement was never made public.

Back in 1961, Connery's girlfriend and future wife, Diane Cilento, had been instrumental in persuading him to take the Bond role in the first place. In the 1980s, it was Connery's second wife, French painter Micheline Roquebrune, who would persuade him to return to the role in *Thunderball*. The court battle over plagiarism had dragged on. Jack Whittingham had withdrawn from the action because he could not afford the legal costs, but Kevin McCrory kept fighting and eventually won his case against Ian Fleming over the use of part of his script.

Sean Connery, always a fan of the underdog, had been amused by the young Irishman's victory over the author and, by default, over the producers in protecting his part-authorship of the story. It meant that when Eon got round to making the movie of the novel in 1965, McCrory was named as producer in the credits and got a share of the profits. It had been a canny move by Broccoli and Saltzman. By bringing McCrory on board as producer of the Eon film, they hoped to protect their franchise from a rival Bond production.

Yet, in the 1980s, McCrory was again looking to exploit his ownership of this bit of Bond by making another film, based loosely on the *Thunderball* storyline. And this time, it would not be as part of the Eon label, but an independent production. When Connery was approached about reviving the character that he had vowed never to play again in an unofficial non-Eon Bond project, he shocked everyone and agreed. At 52, he was probably too old to play the role. But then his replacement, Roger Moore, was three years older than him and he was still playing Bond. It was Micheline who managed to convince her husband to take on the role once more, and she even provided the movie title when she told him: *Never Say Never Again.*

In the 12 years since he last donned the Bond wig, Connery had produced an impressive body of films that showed the range of his acting abilities. He had proved without doubt that he was not just a handsome hunk who looked good in a tux holding a revolver, but the filming of *Never Say Never Again* was not a happy experience and Connery clashed with the director, Irwin Kershner. While training for a stunt scene with a martial arts expert, by the name of Steven Seagal, Sean broke his wrist. He was left so disillusioned by the experience it would be several years before his next film.

Cubby Broccoli took Connery's decision to make a rival Bond movie personally and was hurt by the move. If Connery had been driven to make the film by a desire to prove that Bond didn't need Cubby Broccoli, he failed. The resulting movie was not up to the Eon standards. Cubby at least had the consolation that *Never Say Never Again* lost in the battle of the box office with the 'genuine' Bond movie of that year, *Octopussy*.

One of the roles that would eventually tempt Connery back to work was playing a tough Irish American cop, with a Scottish accent, in the *Untouchables*. It would win him an Oscar for best supporting actor. He still had many of his best and most memorable films ahead of him: *The Rock, The Hunt of Red October, The Russia House, The Name of the Rose* and *Indiana Jones and the Last Crusade.*

Connery stopped making films after *The League of Extraordinary Gentleman* in 2003. He was paid $17 million for the movie. It was another unhappy shooting experience and again he fell out spectacularly with the director. It would be a disaster at the box office. Sean received a Lifetime Achievement Award from the American Film Institute in 2006. He would go on to turn down offers to appear in *The Lord of The Rings* trilogy, as Gandalf, as well as roles in *The Matrix trilogy* and the Harry Potter movies. He put his decision to stop acting down to the 'idiots now making films in Hollywood'.

When still in his thirties, Connery had spoken of his long-term ambitions as an actor: 'I suppose more than anything else, I'd like to be an old man with a good face. Like Hitchcock or Picasso. They've worked hard all their lives, but there's nothing weary about them. They never wasted a day with the sort of nonsense that clutters up life, they know that life is not just a bloody popularity contest.'

He died at his home in Nassau, in the Bahamas, in 2020, aged 90. The obituaries around the globe all spoke of his work as Bond but gave equal measure to the many other films he had made, working with some of the finest directors in Hollywood and England. He had shaken off the curse of being typecast with style. After working together on *Dr No*, Ursula Andress went on to maintain a lifelong friendship with Connery, and he was godfather to her son. 'Sean stayed exactly the same person I met in '62, down to earth and real.' Connery had once said: 'To try and erase the image of Bond is next to impossible.' What he had managed to do, at the end of it all, was to both be defined by the Bond role and to transcend it.

In his last novel published before his death, *You Only Live Twice*, Ian Fleming had filled in details of Bond's biography and background. He gave James Bond a Scottish ancestry. That backstory reflected his own ancestry but the author, who had been so incensed that his quintessentially English agent should be played by a rough, 'overgrown stuntman' from Edinburgh, had, in the end, made Bond an honorary Scot.

At the beginning of the 1960s — before the Bond movies — things had been looking particularly bleak for the two producers. Cubby Broccoli was left pretty much broke after the box office failure of his final Warwick movie, *The Trial of Oscar Wilde*. He'd had even considered quitting Britain altogether and taking his new, young family back to America and trying his luck there. Harry Saltzman's ambition to set the movie world alight with grim English kitchen sink dramas had not really worked out. He had bet his all on optioning the Bond books and, if Broccoli had not come along at the right moment, would have likely lost that bet. But by the middle of the same decade, their fortunes had changed dramatically: they were now the Men with the Golden Franchise. The whole world was going Bond crazy, and they had the exclusive option on virtually all of Fleming's catalogue, as well as the legal right to dream up and film new stories with Fleming's character.

True, there was the annoyance of seeing a rival producer try to cash in on their Bond success with the 1967 parody, *Casino Royale*. However, their rivals had made a huge hash of a film, even with a cast that included Peter Sellers, Woody Allen, Orson Welles, and David Niven, as well as an appearance by Ursula Andress. Among the many writers listed as contributing to the Casino Royale script was Wolf Mankowitz. Perhaps this was the Bond picture he really should have taken his name off.

This was the age of Beatle wigs on sale in Woolworths, and the Bond producers weren't about to miss out on the opportunities to cash in on product tie-ins which gave the fanatical Bond fan some small taste of secret agent glamour. Fleming had been no stranger to product placement. His novels were littered with the brand names, from cars to cigarettes to champagne. However, the writer had vetoed any product tie-ins with Bond which involved toiletries. The producers sought out deals with purveyors of cigarettes and alcohol, bikinis, and motor cars, as well as toy figures and toy cars with ejector seats, spy sets, boxes of magic tricks and board games.

Following the success of *Dr No*, the always evident differences between the two producers were starting to grow ever wider. Cubby now focused all of his energies on the Bond franchise, and he would do that for the remainder of his life. It was an obsession that would turn Bond into a kind of family business. His daughter Barbara was two when she had wandered about on the Jamaican location shoots for *Dr No*. As she grew up, large chunks of her childhood would be spent on location shoots somewhere in the world. As far back as she could remember, she was being tutored on all things producing by her father. Her half-brother, Michael G Wilson, was the product of Dana's previous marriage to Batman actor Lewis Wilson. He would become another part of the family movie firm.

By contrast Harry Saltzman was already displaying signs of restlessness, looking at how he could levy the massive success of Bond into the cornerstone of bigger, wider ambitions to build a movie empire. As part of their deal with UA, Eon were contracted to produce a non-Bond movie. They were offered the opportunity to make a film with a cheeky but lovable bunch of Liverpudlian musicians. Saltzman was scornful of the idea. He just couldn't see the appeal. And why bother with a flash-in-the-pan pop group when you could make a movie with an established, all-round entertainment legend? He reunited with the decidedly un-Fab Bob Hope. The experience of producing *The Iron Petticoat* had obviously been forgotten, or at least forgiven.

Call Me Bwana was a typical Hope vehicle. The comic played a cowardly writer who has passed himself off as a big game hunter, only to be recruited by the US Government as an expert on Africa and to help them find a missing space probe. The production was chaotic, with the script being written and rewritten during the filming. One actress, who had been employed to play a nuclear scientist, learned on the set that her role was now as a secret agent. In a nod to *Dr No*, there was even a scene where Hope's character finds a tarantula crawling up his body. Meanwhile, United Artists made The Beatles' *A Hard Day's Night* with another producer. It was a critical success and even managed to get a couple of Oscar nominations. It also outperformed *Call Me Bwana* at the box office.

What was more of a success for Harry was creating a new secret agent franchise, independent of the Eon brand. Like so many other producers around the world Harry Saltzman was jumping on the Bond wagon with his own rival spy movies, with a determinedly non-Bond secret agent. Saltzman optioned the novels of Len Deighton and his downbeat government agent, creating a run of successful films with Michael Caine in the lead role. In Deighton's novels the agent is not given a name, but on screen he needed one.

Fleming had said that, back in the early 1950s, when choosing what to call his protagonist, he wanted the most boring name he could think of. Now that moniker, James Bond, was synonymous with glamour, excitement and living on the edge. What they wanted for Deighton's character, the anti-Bond, was something really, really dull and flat. It was Harry who thought up the surname Palmer, and Caine chipped in that Harry was a very dull first name, not realising his faux pas until he saw the look of Saltzman's face. Caine would play the role in three successful Harry Palmer films, establishing him as a film star, as well as being the first screen action hero to wear spectacles.

As befitting someone who was sitting on a cinematic equivalent of a goldmine, Harry started living an extravagant movie mogul lifestyle. He bought himself a huge mansion outside of London and would conduct business meeting while sitting on a blow-up chair in the middle of his private swimming pool, even though he couldn't swim.

The volatile temper was still there. Charles 'Jerry' Jeroe, a public relations executive at UA, said: 'Harry was a person who, if he felt you were not doing everything you should, he made it well known and he could really blow up at you.' But while he had that short fuse, the anger would usually pass just as quickly, and, while the people he had railed against would still be upset and tearful, he would have already moved on and completely forgotten about the issue.

Harry travelled around in chauffeur driven Rolls Royce's and started to dress in the most outrageous clothes, even by fashion standards of the decade. His favoured uniform was bright yellow or red pants suits. For good measure, he had two German Shepherd dogs as pets. One was called James and the other Bond. The country house would be crowded with party guests who were the who's who of swinging London, from Roger Moore and Michael Caine to Peter Sellers and Mick Jagger. Any potential Bond girl would be invited to stay in the mansion, where Harry and Jaqueline could assess her potential for the next Bond film.

Always a fan of the plushest and most expensive restaurants, Harry had developed a vexing habit of complaining about the food and sending not just his meal back to the kitchen, but the food of everybody else at the table. As Cubby once said of Harry: 'If he was at the Last Supper, he'd send that back, too'. He was still an active part of the creative production team on the Bond films, coming up with mad ideas. How could they get Bond trapped inside a giant spin dryer? What if Bond wakes up and finds a live crocodile in his bed next to him? 'Harry would spew out like five ideas,' recalls Tom Mankiewicz, 'and two of them were absolutely wonderful and three of them were horrible.'

Meanwhile, he was using the wealth he gained as a producer on the Bond films to invest in new technology and film related companies. He was now a bona fide movie mogul, but what he really wanted was to be a business titan. His son Steven said: 'He got bored quickly. I tell you straight up my father had an attention span problem.' Unfortunately, his unique talents as a producer did not translate into the staid, conservative world of business. Harry lost a lot of money in his various investments and banks were calling in their loans. He tried to get new film projects off the ground in the early seventies but ran into trouble, mainly due to lack of funds. His financial problems eventually became so great they threatened the very existence of Eon and the future production of the Bond films. The crisis further soured his already difficult relationship with Broccoli. After much manoeuvring, and refusing to sell his stake to his partner, he finally sold his share of the business to United Artists for £17.5m in 1975. Eon Productions, the company he had set up with Cubby, remained extant. It's just he was no longer part of it. The volatile partnership between Broccoli and Saltzman had survived nine successive Bond films.

Harry moved to Florida to escape Britain's stringent

new tax laws. His beloved wife Jaqueline became seriously ill, and he cared for her until her death in 1980. He had one last connection to the Bond films. The Israeli actor, Topol, had a role in the 1981 film, *For Your Eyes Only*, and suggested to Cubby that he reach out to his old business partner. Saltzman attended the London premiere of the film and the two producers greeted each other like old friends. 'I know Harry was touched to be there and to feel he was a still part of Bond,' said Roger Moore. 'That was a very nice and a very big gesture from Cubby.'

In his final years, Harry worked on theatre projects, tried to get films off the ground and remarried to Adriana Ghinsberg who, like his beloved Jacqueline, had been a refugee from Romania. They settled in a small village outside Versailles. He died in September 1994 in the American Hospital in Neuilly-sur-Seine, a Paris suburb. The cause was a heart attack. Hilary Saltzman, Harry's daughter said that Connery had been kind and gentlemanly to her, despite his dispute with her father. 'I think this was a business situation that was not going well,' Hilary said of her father's troubled relationship with the actor. 'I think it's a shame that it crossed into their personal relationship.'

'Cubby and Harry were a marvellous team for many reasons,' said Jerry Jeroe. 'They were both creative. They were both innovative. They were both very good businessmen and they really, truly worked well together. They were an odd combination of personalities. Cubby and Harry represented a relationship that was based on two opposing points of view reaching the same objective. They made terrific movies.' Steven Saltzman said: 'I think the best marriages are made from opposites, and I think they both brought a lot to the party.'

The composer Monty Norman agreed: 'They were very good together, but they were chalk and cheese. You had this wonderful Italian-American and Jewish Canadian combination. Harry could be very difficult but Cubby was always a gentleman in every sense of the word. I mean, he could be a tough businessman, but he was truly a lovely man, no question. He really did engender a family atmosphere on set.' Unlike Harry, Cubby was content to devote the rest of his working life in service of the Bond franchise. He would have one further notable deviation from his Bond producing role.

Chitty Chitty Bang Bang was a story about an eccentric family with a magical car that Ian Fleming had written for his son Caspar. A book form of the story was published after his death. Broccoli produced the musical screen version, starring Dick Van Dyke and Lionel Jeffries, in 1968. Broccoli understood that adherence to the Bond formula they had developed early in the films was the key to the longevity of the franchise. He had built around him a trusted crew, of technicians, composers, editors, set designers, actors and directors who would be part of the Bond family, often turning down other film projects just to be back together again on the next location shoot of the next Bond film, wherever in the world that was. And always, Cubby would be there, on set, knowing everyone's name, asking after their partners and children, joining on the long night shoots, cooking up big pots of pasta and doling out meals the crew, with his daughter Barbara and step-son Michael beside him. There were crew members at work on the Craig movies in the 21st century who were the second and third generation family members of people who helped make the Connery films back in the 1960s. That is simply not something that happens on other films.

As the movies continued to be made by the Eon family, the character of James Bond would, at times, be in danger of disappearing into the background as the sets and gadgetry took centre stage. Or the jokes and sly asides would become cartoonish and lame. That would only change, as happened several times during its lifetime, when a new actor came in to play Bond or a new director came on board, and they would correct and realign the Bond legacy.

After the departure of Harry, Cubby continued to have a hands-on role in the Bond films, with Barbara and Michael taking up more and more of the mantle of producers under his watchful eye. Right from the start of the Bond movies, Cubby's wife, Dana, had acted as an unofficial adviser to her husband. She sat in on the production discussions, read the screenplays and, coming from a writing background herself, made key script suggestions. 'Dana is just as involved with the Bond pictures as I am,' Cubby once said. 'Her input has always been valuable, often crucial.'

Cubby won the Irving G Thalberg Memorial Award in recognition of his producing career at the 1981 Oscars. He was awarded an OBE in the UK as well as the French Commander des Arts et Les Lettres. The Albert R Broccoli 007 Stage, at Pinewood Studios, is one of the largest sound stages in the world. Ken Adam had created it to accommodate the interior of the supertanker in *The Spy Who Loved Me*. It cost $1.8 million to build, and was intended to be a temporary structure, but then they found other film makers were keen to use it.

Former British Prime Minister Harold Wilson, Roger Moore and other Bond actors attended the christening of the stage, in December 1976, carried out by Dana breaking a bottle of champagne over one of the submarines used in the film. Cubby had come a long way from the young penniless man who turned up in Hollywood to visit his mob-connected cousin.

It shouldn't be surprising that Hollywood filmmakers and organised crime would find themselves bedfellows at so many turns of the past century. After all, both were in the entertainment industry. One was dealing in, during the prohibition years, alcohol and then moving into prostitution, drugs and gambling. The other's currency was big screen escape and people's fantasies. Since its inception, Hollywood has always shared a mutual fascination with the bad guys, the mobsters, the booze runners. The Hays Code, introduced in the 1930s, was designed to combat films that promoted or glamourised sex or any amoral behaviour. Which meant that all the gangsters, as played by Cagney, Robinson, Raft and Bogart, would necessarily come to a bad end in the final reel. But that was only after they had thrilled audiences with their crimes, promiscuity, and general amorality.

In both industries, many of the major players were émigrés or the children of émigrés who arrived in America with nothing. These were men with no access to opportunity or education, who would, by their own efforts, become wildly rich and powerful in tough, unforgiving industries.

The mobsters were attracted to Hollywood because it was another opportunity to make money, or at least coerce money out of the studios, as well as hang out with biggest celebrities of the day and, often, sleep with some of the world's most beautiful women. It gave them a veneer of respectability and even celebrity. And they found the studios and their movie star 'friends' were easy marks for extracting money.

For the Hollywood set, steeped in portrayals of fake hardmen and pretend machine guns, the mobsters were the real deal. They got a kick out of hanging out with them, using them as source material, sometimes leaning on them to sort out problems in their career or just enjoying the vicarious thrill of partying with killers and gangsters.

These Mob connections could both cause — and then solve — any labour disputes that might threaten a production. They could provide unique solutions to disputes between stars and studios.

That close relationship was a truth when Cubby's cousin Pat muscled himself into the role of bit player in the film world of the 1930s, or when Ben Hecht had to have his Scarface script run past goons sent by Al Capone for approval. It was still there in the 1950s, when Lana Turner wasn't the only movie star to get too close to these violent and dangerous men. When the Mafia created Las Vegas out of the desert, Hollywood was an essential part of the mix. Most of the major studios found it wise to invest in these new fun palaces. Their biggest stars jetted down and provided the glamour at the tables, or else paid for their supper by signing contract agreeing to lengthy seasons of live performances at the glitzy venues. There was a reason why studio bosses like Harry Cohn at Columbia and Jack Warner at Warner Bros openly wore 'friendship rings' gifted to them by the crime bosses. Jack Warner may not have understood the English as spoken in Saltzman's *Look Back in Anger* film, but he certainly understood every word when these men started talking to him.

Cubby would not be the only Hollywood player whose life and career would, almost by necessity, skirt the grey area between these two parallel worlds. Sidney Korshak, a Chicago lawyer, was perhaps the perfect synapse of these two worlds. Through his law practise, Korshak came into contact with Chicago mobsters including Al Capone. Korshak would go on to become a power player and 'fixer' in Hollywood, specialising in labour consultations and negotiations. His client list ran from the notorious union boss Jimmy Hoffa and various mobsters to more respectable clients like MCA/Universal studios, Hilton

GAMBLERS, BEFORE THEY DIE, ARE OFTEN GIVEN A GREAT GOLDEN STREAK OF LUCK

Hotels and *Playboy*. He was friends with everyone, from Ronald Reagan to Warren Beatty, producer Robert Evans to *Playboy*'s Hugh Hefner. Few people outside Hollywood would recognise his name or his face, but that was all part of his power. He was too important, too big, for the gossip columns and tabloid rags. According to Evans, Korshak conducted all business orally and always had a large supply of nickels to make calls from pay telephones that were less likely to be tapped by the FBI. He was, allegedly, one of the few people who knew what really happened to Jimmy Hoffa. Korshak had been named by the FBI as 'the most powerful lawyer in the world' because of his mob connections. Yet, despite all the links and all the stories swirling around him, no indictment or criminal charges were ever laid against him. He had his own table at Le Bistro, a Beverly Hills restaurant in which he owned a share, and among his regular lunch time guests was his good friend, Cubby Broccoli.

When the Bond franchise moved to Las Vegas as the backdrop to Connery's last Eon Bond film, *Diamonds Are Forever*, Sidney acted as a kind of unofficial adviser. Set designer Ken Adam remembers: 'The connection that Cubby had that allowed us to do some very interesting filming was somebody called Sidney Korshak. I had lunch with Sidney in a bistro in Beverly Hills. The next day I flew to Vegas and was met by a big black limo and was shown any house I wanted to look at.' For good measure Sidney suggested casting actress Jill St John, allegedly his lover at the time, as the film's lead Bond girl, diamond smuggler Tiffany Case.

Mankiewicz was on the set in Las Vegas and got to meet Korshak. When the screenwriter casually mentioned he had to go back to New York for a couple of days and was having trouble booking a hotel room, Korshak made him a generous offer. He had a suite at the Carlyle Hotel that was empty and he could stay there. A grateful Mankiewicz accepted. Later, when Broccoli learned of this, he came to the writer: 'Listen, let me give you some advice. Sidney's a great friend of mine, he likes you very much. Don't ever let Sidney do you a favour. I'm serious.' Sidney Korshak was not someone you wanted to be in debt to.

Cubby's persona remained the friendly, lovable producer on the set, but the affability cloaked a steely resolve and fierce ambition. As he said himself: 'You don't get to be the world's richest producer without biting a few heads off. It's a dog-eat-dog business. I don't think I'm difficult. You just have to remind people you're there.'

Cubby always insisted every film include Ian Fleming's name in the credits, even if it was a completely new Bond story. The production searched for film titles that at least had some Fleming connection, such as the last film Cubby would have a hand in, *Goldeneye*, named after Fleming's Jamaican hideaway.

In 1995, Cubby was seriously ill but insisted on viewing the footage from the still-in-production *Goldeneye*. Before he died, he and Connery were able to briefly reconnect. 'They acknowledged that what they had done together was very special,' said Barbara Broccoli. 'I'm happy that they made peace. We have a lot to thank Sean Connery for.'

Cubby Broccoli died in Beverly Hills in June 1996, at the age of 87. Since his passing all the subsequent Bond films continue to say 'Albert R Broccoli Eon Productions Presents'. Cubby had carefully mentored his stepson and daughter into the roles of keeping a firm hand on the production of the movies after he was gone.

Barbara summed up the achievements of the team that first brought Bond to the big screen: 'The original filmmakers were Cubby and Harry, Ian Fleming, Terence

GAMBLERS, BEFORE THEY DIE, ARE OFTEN GIVEN A GREAT GOLDEN STREAK OF LUCK

Young and Sean Connery. They all created something extraordinary. They changed cinema history. They pushed the envelope. Look at the way those films were made. I mean Ken Adam; he changed the look of cinema. Peter Hunt, the editor, changed editing. They did something revolutionary, and I think whenever you create something together, it's a tragedy when you split up. Like a marriage, it's the child that matters, and the child in this case is the extraordinary legacy.'

Before he died, Cubby cautioned Barbara and Michael to protect the Bond legacy: 'Don't let 'em screw it up.'

Bibliography

When Harry Met Cubby: The Story of the James Bond Producers by Robert Sellers, The History Press

Some Kind of Hero: The Remarkable Story of the James Bond Films by Matthew Field and Ajay Chowdhury, The History Press

The James Bond Bedside Companion by Raymond Benson, Boxtree

Kiss Kiss Bang! Bang!: The Unofficial James Bond Film Companion by Alan Barnes, Batsford

John Barry: A Sixties Theme, From James Bond To Midnight Cowboy by Eddi Fiegel, Constable

Noël Coward by Clive Fisher, Weidenfeld & Nicolson

The Dark Heart of Hollywood: Glamour, Guns and Gambling – Inside the Mafia's Global Empire Paperback by Douglas Thompson

For Your Eyes Only: Behind the Scenes of the James Bond Films by David Giammarco, ECW Press

Agent Zigzag by Ben Macintyre, Bloomsbury Publishing

Ian Fleming: The Man Behind James Bond Hardcover by Andrew Lycett, Turner Publishing

Sean Connery: The Measure of a Man by Christopher Bray, Faber and Faber

Firefly: Noël Coward in Jamaica Hardcover by Chris Salewicz and Adrian Boot

The Noël Coward Diaries, edited by Graham Payn and Sheridan Morley, Papermac

Dr No by Ian Fleming Vintage Classics

Casino Royale by Ian Fleming Vintage

From Russia With Love by Ian Fleming, Vintage

You Only Live Twice by Ian Fleming, Vintage

Sean Connery, a Biography by Michael Freedland, Orion

Sir Sean Connery, 1930–2020, The Definitive Biography by John Parker, John Blake

Peter Fleming by Duff Hart-Davis, Oxford University Press